# WHATEVER YOU DO, BE HAPPY

Adams Media
An Imprint of Simon & Schuster, Inc.
57 Littlefield Street
Avon, Massachusetts 02322

First Adams Media hardcover edition
April 2020

ADAMS MEDIA and colophon are trademarks
of Simon & Schuster.

For information about special discounts for
bulk purchases, please contact Simon &
Schuster Special Sales at 1-866-506-1949
or business@simonandschuster.com.

The Simon & Schuster Speakers Bureau
can bring authors to your live event. For more
information or to book an event contact the
Simon & Schuster Speakers Bureau at
1-866-248-3049 or visit our website at
www.simonspeakers.com.

Interior design, illustrations, and hand lettering
by Priscilla Yuen

Manufactured in the United States of America

10  9  8  7  6  5  4  3  2  1

Library of Congress Cataloging-in-Publication
Data
Names: Dellitt, Julia, author.
Title: Whatever you do, be happy / Julia Dellitt.
Description: Avon, Massachusetts:
Adams Media, 2020.
Includes index.
Identifiers: LCCN 2019059304 |
ISBN 9781507213476 (hc) |
ISBN 9781507213483 (ebook)
Subjects: LCSH: Mind and body. |
Self-actualization (Psychology) | Happiness.
Classification: LCC BF161 .D375 2020 |
DDC 158.1--dc23
LC record available at
https://lccn.loc.gov/2019059304

ISBN 978-1-5072-1347-6
ISBN 978-1-5072-1348-3 (ebook)

# WHATEVER YOU DO, BE HAPPY

## 400 Things to Think & Do for A HAPPY LIFE

### JULIA DELLITT

**ADAMS MEDIA**

New York  London  Toronto  Sydney  New Delhi

# INTRODUCTION

Sometimes life throws you a curveball, or you just feel like you woke up on the wrong side of the bed—and that's okay! Everyone has bad days when happiness feels out of reach. And sure, you can't always control what happens, but you *can* control how you react to it. Every day is an opportunity to shift your mindset to a happier, more positive place.

And that's where *Whatever You Do, Be Happy* comes in! Here, you'll find four hundred easy, mood-boosting activities to help you find joy—no matter where you are or what might be bothering you—including:

- Throwing a solo dance party
- Re-evaluating your priorities
- Listening to an inspiring podcast
- Setting a boundary
- Thanking an old teacher

You'll also find a number of inspirational quotes throughout the book to shake up your beliefs around happiness and remind you that you're not alone. Anytime your mind, heart, or spirit need a quick lift, flip through to an activity or quote that resonates with you. Then feel the stress and negativity slip away!

You might think of happiness as coming with important milestones—graduating from school, going on a first date, nailing a job interview—and that's true, but it is also about the little things you do for yourself, like taking your dog for a walk, listening to a favorite playlist, or reading a great book. It's time to start taking charge of your happiness. Are you ready to get started?

### CELEBRATE FOR NO REASON

Don't wait for a special occasion to celebrate your life! Pop open a bottle of sparkling cider on a random Monday. Grab a bunch of colorful balloons at the grocery store and let them loose around your apartment. Keep a packet of "just-in-case" confetti on hand to toss on a whim. Use any day as an excuse to toast yourself.

### KEEP A TALISMAN WITHIN REACH

Talismans are like lucky charms: They carry good vibes wherever they go. Keep your own personal talisman nearby for whenever you need a happiness boost. It could be a stress ball you squeeze when trying to come up with a creative idea, a keychain inscribed with a favorite quote that makes you smile, or a crystal that has certain healing properties.

### STOP TO SMELL THE ROSES

Did you know flowers are nature's way of triggering the release of dopamine in your brain? When you see their bright colors and inhale those fragrant scents, it creates an immediate, positive effect on your mood. So the next time you need a little lift, pick up a bouquet of wildflowers at the farmers' market, or pause at your neighbor's lilac bush.

It's been my experience that you can nearly always enjoy things if you make up your mind firmly that you will.

**LUCY MAUD MONTGOMERY,**
author of *Anne of Green Gables*

When our body language is **CONFIDENT AND OPEN,** other people respond in kind, unconsciously reinforcing not only their perception of us but also our perception of ourselves.

**AMY CUDDY,**
author of *Presence: Bringing Your Boldest Self to Your Biggest Challenges*

# STRIKE A POSE

Did you know that the way you hold your body can influence how you feel about yourself? It's true! According to social psychologist Amy Cuddy, "power posing" (adjusting your body language to be open) creates a mental association to assertiveness and self-confidence. In other words, when you take up space, like holding your arms and legs away from your body, it nudges your attitude to follow suit. Seem a little too good to be true? Maybe, but it's not: Just sitting or standing up straight leads to a better mood.

Cuddy's favorite power poses include Wonder Woman (standing with your feet apart, your hands on your hips, and your chin tilted up) and The Loomer (leaning forward slightly while standing). The Wonder Woman is great for giving yourself a little boost in confidence, while The Loomer helps you better show others that you are listening to what they are saying.

So, the next time you're feeling down in the dumps, check in: Are your shoulders hunched up toward your ears as you walk, or rounded forward over your phone screen while you shoot off that text message? Drop them down and slightly back, and pull your belly button in toward your spine to tighten those core muscles (that counts as a workout, right?). Next, while putting equal weight on each foot, reach your arms up over your head (for an extra mood boost, imagine you're a rock star onstage) to stack your head over your shoulders, and your hips over your ankles. Feels better, right?

## WALK AROUND THE BLOCK

You get home after a long day and you're feeling overwhelmed. Before reaching for that bag of chips and the TV remote, head outside for a quick walk around the block! Taking a walk is one of the fastest ways to reset your mood. Your body experiences a "moving meditation" while walking that allows you to clear your mind, look around (instead of at a screen!), and feel more energized—which in turn will lead to a happier mindset. It doesn't need to be a long walk either: Experts say just ten to fifteen minutes will do the trick. The best part? Walking is accessible, free, and you don't need any fancy equipment.

## ELIMINATE CLUTTER

A messy home can easily become a big source of stress, which is one of the main obstacles that can get between you and feeling happy. Those stacks of books on the desk, random cereal boxes on the table, and piles of clean laundry in need of folding add up—and start to weigh on you. Spend some time tidying one room in your living space, whether it's the living room, kitchen, or bedroom. You can even start with a specific task or section of the room, taking it one thing at a time until you've got a clean, organized space. Not only will this create more room for happiness to grow, but it can also make life a bit easier in the long run. No more frantic searches for your car keys when you should be heading out the door!

### DRINK A GLASS OF MILK

You probably already know that milk is full of essential nutrients that benefit your health, like calcium, protein, potassium, and tons of vitamins. But what might surprise you is that it can also help reduce stress, improve your memory, and boost your mood.

### PRACTICE THE THREE-TO-ONE RATIO

Psychologist Dr. Barbara Fredrickson created the three-to-one ratio for happiness: For every negative moment you experience, you should try to experience three positive ones. Sometimes things go wrong, but carving out time for three positive experiences can make you feel happier in the wake of those less-than-desirable outcomes.

### COMPLIMENT A STRANGER

Being kind to someone makes you feel like a nice person, sure, but it also can have a huge effect on your happiness. After all, pointing out the positives in others is a great way to start seeing more of the positives in yourself—and the world around you. Plus, by putting yourself out there, you improve your conversational skills!

Sometimes you have to

**DISCONNECT** to stay **CONNECTED.**

Remember the old days when you had eye contact

during a conversation? When everyone wasn't

looking down at a device in their hands?

We've become so focused on that tiny screen

that we forget the big picture,

*THE PEOPLE RIGHT IN FRONT OF US.*

**REGINA BRETT,** journalist

# TURN OFF YOUR PHONE

Many of us treat our phone like it's a limb we couldn't live without; it's always in our pocket when walking around, mounted next to the steering wheel while driving... You've probably got your phone on you right now. And hey, there's a lot to love about it: instant connections to your friends, easy directions to that new burrito place, quick answers to just about any question—you get it.

Still, it's important to take breaks from screen time. You've already heard about some of the benefits of disconnecting: better sleep habits, improved communication skills, increased productivity—just to name a few. But there's also a major one you might not have considered: It can make you feel happier! Turning off your phone for even a short thirty-minute break from mindlessly scrolling through that *Instagram* feed means avoiding the "comparison trap" (subconsciously comparing your own life to the picture-perfect lives you see on social media). It also means more free time to enjoy the present without any distractions—whether that's through an IRL conversation with a loved one, or a fun solo hobby.

Want to take things up a notch? Try leaving your phone at home for an entire day while you're at work or out with friends, or turn it off for a whole weekend of quality "me time."

## HAVE A SOLO DANCE PARTY

Want to turn your mood around in a couple of minutes? Throw on your favorite happy song for a mini dance party! Dancing reduces stress hormones and releases feel-good endorphins—no dressing up (or leaving the house) required. So bust a move in your pajamas while drinking your morning coffee, jump around the second you get home from a long day, or shake your shoulders at a red light on your way to the store.

## ASK YOURSELF IF IT WILL MATTER NEXT YEAR

When worry or stress about something gets in the way of feeling happy, ask yourself if it will matter in a year. Skipping a workout? Probably not. Getting stuck in traffic? Not likely. It's all about perspective, as well as how you choose to spend your energy, time, and attention. In other words, don't sweat the small stuff.

## GO TO BED

Here's the simple truth: A good night's sleep can solve many, many problems. When you're overtired, you're more likely to feel moody and prone to frustration. So on those days where everything seems to be going wrong, or you're struggling with negative feelings, hit the hay early for an easy refresh.

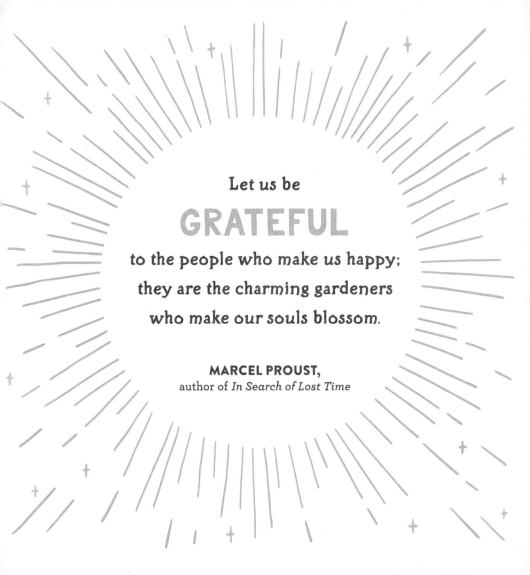

Let us be

# GRATEFUL

to the people who make us happy;
they are the charming gardeners
who make our souls blossom.

**MARCEL PROUST,**
author of *In Search of Lost Time*

## PLAY SELF-CARE CATCH-UP

Choose one day where you truly prioritize self-care, and make it a recurring part of your routine. Maybe Monday nights are your evening for reality TV shows and ice cream. Or one hour every other Wednesday is reserved for meeting with a counselor. Or you start every Sunday with a jog around the neighborhood. Self-care is an important part of cultivating a happy, healthy you.

## BE QUIET

Small doses of silence have the power to completely transform your mood. When you talk less, you listen more: You appreciate the different noises around you, or the task in front of you. And you learn that being quiet creates much-needed space in this very noisy world—space for happiness to pour in, be it through reflecting on the little, beautiful things, or creating something new.

## ROLL YOUR SHOULDERS

Sitting in front of a computer, driving a car, and constantly looking down at a cell phone are all activities that do a number on your shoulders over time, leading to aches and pains that make it hard to relax and enjoy the moment. An easy solution? Sit up tall, and, as you breathe in, roll your shoulders all the way up toward your ears. As you exhale, let them roll down and back.

## LISTEN TO AN UPBEAT SONG

Listening to happy music absolutely makes you feel happier—it's a no-brainer. Upbeat tunes encourage you to remember positive memories (often ones that are linked to particular songs) and also help you see the positives in the present moment. So turn up the music!

## GIVE YOURSELF A HUG

When you're feeling low or in need of some love, giving yourself a squeeze is one of the simplest ways to lift your mood. After all, physical touch releases a dose of oxytocin: a hormone with antidepressant-like effects. Reach your hands for opposite shoulders and wrap your arms around your body, then hug yourself tightly. Stay in that position until the happy feels take hold.

## VISIT THE LIBRARY

Going to your local public library is completely free, and gives you access to all kinds of books, magazines, and other media to stretch your mind. Not only will you feel a little smarter, you'll also feel more connected to your community, and energized by the thrill of hunting through the aisles for an interesting new read. Many libraries even have additional programming and activities such as writing seminars and author events. You can learn something new—or find a quiet nook to kick up your feet and relax with a book.

Everybody has to leave,

everybody has to leave their home

and come back so they can love

it again for all new reasons.

**DONALD MILLER,**
author of *Through Painted Deserts:
Light, God, and Beauty on the Open Road*

# TRAVEL SOMEWHERE NEW

Traveling is one of the best ways to bring more joy into your life. Not only do you get to explore new places and meet new people, but you also walk away with great stories to share later (that time you saw an elephant up close and personal) and to think back on fondly. After all, good old-fashioned nostalgia brings on the happy feels, and also encourages a sense of connection and creativity. And you don't have to drop the big bucks on an international plane ticket or backpack across the globe to make it happen (though you definitely can if you choose to!). You can take a mini road trip with friends to another corner of your region, or maximize a family vacation.

Travel provides a break from your usual routine, which can help you appreciate those "ordinary" days—and your home—more once you return. Seeking out new places also teaches you about yourself: You may discover that you love the adventure of not knowing what will happen next, or the charm of chatting up a seatmate on the bus.

## SEND SOMEONE FLOWERS

Flowers are usually reserved for special occasions, but why wait for birthdays and anniversaries to bring a little dose of happiness to someone's day (and your own too)? Send a brightly colored bouquet to a friend, partner, or family member for no reason at all—other than to show you're thinking of them.

## SET A TIMER FOR A BAD MOOD

The goal of happiness isn't necessarily to completely eliminate negative emotions. It's okay—and normal!—to feel upset at times. But you don't want those more difficult emotions to weigh you down forever, or knock you into a self-defeating spiral. That's where setting a timer on your mood can help: It gives you a specific amount of time to linger in those negative feelings. When the alarm sounds, you know it's time to take a breath and move on. It may sound difficult at first, but the concrete time frame and deliberate act of setting the timer will help you to do so. So when you're feeling sad, mad, or stressed, set a timer on your phone for two minutes and think or journal about everything related to the emotion. Once the timer goes off, you'll be better able to hit the reset button on your mood and welcome in the good things around you.

### ADMIRE A PAINTING

Looking at art, whether at a gallery or museum, or even in someone's home or online, improves your mood. Some research even indicates looking at beautiful art is akin to falling in love, due to the release of dopamine in your brain. Take some time to examine a painting, sculpture, or other piece of art.

### CHECK OUT A NEW PART OF TOWN

Exploring a new part of your town is a surefire way to add a splash of novelty and fun to your routine. Check out a neighborhood you're not familiar with, or visit a local museum to learn about your city's history or claims to fame.

### CHEW MINT GUM

According to a 2010 study, chewing gum can make you feel less anxious, especially if it's a mint variety. The physical act of chewing on a piece of gum improves your concentration and the way your brain manages stress, while the refreshing scent of mint stimulates your ability to focus. Stress aside, you'll be able to enjoy the present and better appreciate the good things in your life.

Life is made up of small pleasures.

Happiness is made up of those tiny successes.

The big ones come too infrequently. And if

you don't collect all these tiny successes,

the big ones don't really mean anything.

**NORMAN LEAR,**
TV writer and producer

# COUNT THE TINY SUCCESSES

Have you ever made a checklist of the little accomplishments in your day? Made lunch—check. Didn't flip out while on hold with customer service—check. Took out the trash—check. It's beyond satisfying to cross things off a list, no matter how small—especially when you've been procrastinating a larger task that requires more time and energy. Yes, you are essentially tricking yourself into being productive...and it's an approach that comes highly recommended by experts! Here's why: Recording your progress boosts your self-confidence. And when you feel more capable of getting stuff done, you're more likely to keep going toward those bigger goals.

Celebrating small wins also gives your body a shot of dopamine, making you feel happier. Maybe you're trying to cut down on sugar, so you write that you swapped that giant, frothy coffee drink for a simple iced cold brew. Check! Or you remembered to wash your favorite outfit on the day of an important meeting—yay! You can treat yourself for these wins, like buying a fancy new notebook after meeting a tight deadline, or simply feel happy in the moment, like when you're having a fantastic hair day and run into your crush.

## LEARN HOW TO PLAY A SONG

Piano, guitar, keyboard—no matter your instrument of choice, it's pretty easy to learn how to play a basic song in a matter of days. If you don't have access to an instrument at home, see if a friend has one you can borrow, or if a local music store will let you practice on one of their models. Then, check out books, video tutorials, or free online lessons to learn how to play a simple song. You can even enlist a tutor to help you master some beginner-level chords and chord progressions. Set a goal to learn how to play a favorite song or popular classic; once you nail the song, you can put on a little concert for your close friends or family to show off your skills—and get an extra boost of happy feelings from your new achievement!

## DRAW

Drawing isn't reserved for professional artists: Anyone can grab a pencil, pen, crayon, or marker and have fun doodling a simple design or practicing a complicated portrait. Animals can be an easy place to start if you are a beginner: The dogs, cats, and birds you likely see on a daily basis are made up of simple geometric shapes. Try starting with a basic cartoon and work your way up to a realistic sketch of your furry friend. You can also find tons of online tutorials and step-by-step guides to help you along the way. As you draw, you'll be using both sides of your brain (the left side to focus on making sure your drawing appears correct, and the right side as your creativity comes out), which releases feel-good endorphins in your brain.

### MAKE EYE CONTACT

Looking someone in the eye is a nonverbal way of asserting yourself and showing self-confidence (even if you're faking it at first). Anytime you're in a conversation, try to make sustained eye contact rather than looking down or around the room. It builds trust and positions you as a leader. It also makes you (and the person you're looking at) happier, because it strengthens your connection and indicates your complete presence with each other.

### HOLD THE DOOR

One simple act of kindness that can bring others—and you—a bit of happiness? Holding the door for someone. You'll feel good about being helpful and considerate, and they'll appreciate the gesture—and may pass it on.

### CHANT "OM"

"Om"—which sounds like "A-U-M"—is an ancient Sanskrit word that symbolizes the existence of all life, and in yoga is viewed as the natural vibration of the earth. Sit up tall, take a big breath in, and as you slowly exhale, let the sacred sound of "om" come out of your throat as if it's vibrating through your entire body. Notice the calming, centering effects during the chant, and the uplift in your mood afterward.

## CHANGE YOUR WALLPAPER

What you see influences how you feel! Update the background, wallpaper, or screensaver of your electronic devices with a picture (or different pictures) that make you happy every time you look at it. Maybe it's a picture of a beautiful forest during fall, a beach with white sand, a bunch of adorable puppies, or a photo of loved ones.

## CLOSE YOUR EYES

You might not have time for a full nap, but you can easily fit in a couple of seconds to close your eyes for a mental reset. Doing so relaxes your mind and gives your brain a break from constantly processing information and visual cues, ultimately boosting your mood. Take a deep breath when your eyes are closed for even more restoration.

## TELL A JOKE

Laughter makes you happier...*and* healthier (for instance, it can lower your blood pressure and risk of heart disease!). A well-timed joke helps you bond and enjoy yourself with others, instantly improving your mood.

The purpose of our life needs to be positive. We weren't born with the purpose of causing trouble, harming others. For our life to be of value, I think we must develop basic good human qualities—warmth, kindness, compassion. Then our life becomes more meaningful and more peaceful—HAPPIER.

**THE 14TH DALAI LAMA,**
spiritual leader and author of *The Art of Happiness*

## CHOOSE TO LET IT GO

Some of the hardest things you'll ever do involve letting go—of things, places, past hurts, expectations, and more. However, when you cling to things that make you feel bad or no longer benefit you, you leave less space for the things that will help you grow and feel happy. For example, instead of constantly dwelling on a past breakup, make the conscious decision to let it go and move on. To help you do this, you can even say it out loud: "I choose to let go of this, because it is only weighing me down." You can also do something symbolic to initiate letting go, like writing the thing down on a piece of paper and then tearing it up. It doesn't mean you won't feel sad or angry or confused by a situation or person again, but you're deciding to take control of your emotions going forward.

## DRINK A GLASS OF WATER WITH LEMON

You already know water is good for your health, but let's be honest: Sometimes plain $H_2O$ is a little boring! Mix things up by infusing your water with lemon. It will help you drink more water, and provide an extra dose of vitamin C. Best of all, it will help you quash fatigue, increase your energy levels, and improve your mood. If you're not a fan of citrus, try infusing with a handful of fresh strawberries or raspberries, or a combination of cucumber and mint, for a delicious, revitalizing way to stay hydrated.

### TAKE A MAGNESIUM SUPPLEMENT

Research suggests magnesium helps reduce feelings of depression, as well as increase your energy levels and improve your sleep habits. It also helps regulate hormones, for an all-around better mood. Not a fan of supplements? Snack on something high in magnesium, like whole-wheat bread, dark chocolate, spinach, and avocado.

### OPEN A WINDOW

Fresh air does the mind and body good—especially if you're typically cooped up inside all day. In fact, fresh air can actually make you feel more energized than a cup of coffee. Pop open a window to help circulate stale air out of your space and lift your mood.

### LIFT WEIGHTS

Strength training—even just a couple of quick sets with hand weights—is a sure-fire way to feel better fast. How? Endorphins: These wonderful hormones boost your mood every single time, especially as a result of exercise. Lifting weights can also help you feel good about your body and its capabilities, as well as your overall appearance.

Usually the things

we think we need become

# THE VERY THINGS

we need a break from.

**JEN HATMAKER,**
author of *The 7 Experiment:
Staging Your Own Mutiny Against Excess*

# LIVE WITH LESS

Minimalism (think capsule wardrobes and Marie Kondo) has become popular, and for good reason: It is a simple way to experience the happiness of feeling truly content with what you have, rather than focusing on what you don't have. Of course, there's nothing wrong with owning stuff, or buying something you want; it only becomes problematic when you begin to assign too much meaning to material things, or find yourself getting caught up in always having the latest and greatest.

In her book, Jen Hatmaker describes a seven-month experiment in which she made intentional choices to embrace minimalism. She wore the same seven articles of clothing for a given month, ate the same seven foods, gave away seven things each day, got rid of seven forms of media (TV, *Twitter*, radio, etc.), adopted seven sustainable habits, spent money in the same seven places, and took seven pauses a day to reflect on all of these choices. At the end of the experiment, she found that practicing minimalism helped her focus on the stuff she truly cared most about. It was a freeing experience that brought more happiness into her life.

Okay, so Hatmaker's approach is a bit extreme, but you don't need to commit to a lifestyle overhaul to reap the benefits of living with less. You can simply cut down on the number of streaming services you subscribe to, own three pairs of jeans instead of eight, or get rid of that second set of measuring cups you never use.

### GET A FULL NIGHT'S SLEEP

Experts agree: More sleep leads to more happiness. Prioritizing six to eight hours of shut-eye per night helps with your attention span, ability to remember things, and decision-making skills, as well as your overall mood. Adjust your schedule so you can get a revitalizing amount of sleep every night.

### PICK A HAPPY SOUND

From calls and calendar reminders to emails and text messages—your phone is constantly pinging with new notifications. Rather than a boring buzz or ding, change the notification sound to something uplifting or funny; every time your phone goes off, you'll feel the urge to smile.

### SET AN INTENTION FOR THE DAY

How you approach your day affects how you feel throughout it. Set an intention each day that helps you focus on positive thoughts and feelings. Deciding "I am going to have a positive attitude" goes a long way, especially in those less-than-wonderful moments, like when a driver cuts you off in traffic.

### SAY A SILLY WORD IN A GRUMPY VOICE

Guess what: It's really hard to stay in a bad mood when you use a funny voice to talk about it. No, really! The next time you're feeling cranky, say it in a silly way—very slowly in a soft whisper, loudly and dramatically like you're an actor in a play, or with a bad accent. Chances are high you'll start smiling.

### DARE TO DREAM

It's way easy to worry about the worst possible thing that might happen when you're facing the unknown. Instead, challenge yourself to imagine what the best-case scenario looks like. You can even close your eyes to focus on every little detail of the ideal outcome. Not only is it an instant mood-booster, but it also reminds you to think positively more often in your daily life.

### PLACE YOUR HAND ON YOUR HEART

If you find yourself feeling stressed or down in the dumps, take a second to put your hand over your heart. Feel your heartbeat, and use it as a reminder of the fact that you are alive. Through all of your struggles and triumphs, your body is working hard to keep you here, and that's something worth celebrating.

## READ A BIOGRAPHY

Anytime you're hyper-focused on what seems to be going wrong in your own life, it can help to get out of your head by reading about somebody else's life. You'll discover lessons from their experiences and may feel comforted in learning that someone else has dealt with some of the same problems you are going through. Yep, famous people (even from hundreds of years ago) also experience ups and downs—you're not alone!

## SCREAM

It might seem a little odd, but screaming can be super therapeutic, especially if you're feeling overwhelmed. There's something about the physical act of releasing tension—and honestly, doing something that you might feel you're not "supposed" to do—that takes the edge off and lifts your spirits. Just be sure you don't alarm anyone around you; head outside or yell into a pillow.

## FORGIVE SOMEONE

It's normal to feel upset when someone hurts or angers you. However, when you hold on to that pain or frustration, it becomes a weight that moves with you from day to day, keeping you from truly feeling happy. Release that weight by making the decision to forgive them and move on.

We tend to forget that happiness doesn't come as a result of getting something we don't have, but rather of recognizing and appreciating what we do have.

———

**FRIEDRICH KOENIG,** inventor

Breathing in, I calm my body.

Breathing out, I smile.

Dwelling in the present moment,

I know this is a wonderful moment!...

Feelings come and go like clouds in a windy sky.

**CONSCIOUS BREATHING IS MY ANCHOR.**

**THÍCH NHẤT HẠNH,**
spiritual leader, poet, and author of *Stepping into Freedom:
An Introduction to Buddhist Monastic Training*

# PRACTICE ALTERNATE NOSTRIL BREATHING

Pranayama, or breathwork, is a central element of yoga often used at the beginning or end of a physical yoga practice or meditation. Even though it might seem a little unusual to "practice" breathing (after all, it's something you do day in and day out without thinking twice), different exercises with your breath can be beneficial to your emotional well-being. One specific breathing exercise called *Nadi Shodhana*, or "alternate nostril breathing," serves as a powerful tool for reducing anxiety and clearing your mind for a more relaxed, happy mood.

Follow these easy steps to give it a try:

1 Find a comfortable place to sit with your legs crossed.
2 Bring your right hand up, palm toward your face, in front of your nose.
3 Inhale deeply through your nose, then use your pinkie finger to close your left nostril.
4 Exhale slowly through your right nostril.
5 Before your next inhale, let go of your left nostril and use your thumb to close your right nostril.
6 Inhale through your left nostril.
7 Continue alternating nostrils as you inhale and exhale, keeping a slow pace. As you alternate and breathe, notice how your mood changes. (If you feel lightheaded or agitated, stop the practice and explore other forms of breathwork that might be a better fit for you.)

### LINGER IN A BUBBLE BATH

Chilling out in a warm bath, whether you prefer bubbles or not, can help you decompress and feel better—especially right before bed. It's also a nice way to enjoy some quiet downtime solo. You can read a magazine or book, sip on something delicious, play a little music, or even add a couple drops of essential oils in the water for a luxe touch.

### GO FOR A BIKE RIDE

Whether you hop on a bike to hit the trails or prefer an indoor spinning class, any type of bike ride is good for your body—and your mood. One study also found that a short ride reduces stress—so try it out!

### TAKE AN ENNEAGRAM TEST

The Enneagram test is a personality questionnaire that uses your answers to a series of questions to find out which of nine unique personality types you are. Once you know what type you are, you can read more about how that type views the world, their strengths and weaknesses, and their emotional patterns—all of which help you better understand who you are and what makes you happy. In fact, the test can shed light on how you measure happiness in general.

When I was five years old, my mother always told me that happiness was the key to life. When I went to school, they asked me what I wanted to be when I grew up. I wrote down "happy." They told me I didn't understand the assignment, and I told them they didn't understand life.

Unknown

## TALK TO YOURSELF KINDLY

The way you speak to yourself matters, especially since it's so easy to be your own worst critic. It influences how you feel about yourself, and your life. First, notice the ongoing dialogue happening in your mind, or any negative thoughts you're having about yourself. Next, practice positive self-talk. For example, if you make a mistake, your initial thought might be, "That was stupid." Try to add more context and positivity to the reaction: "...but mistakes happen and I'll handle it differently next time." You're only human, after all! Practice talking to yourself the way you would a best friend: with plenty of kindness and understanding. Why should you deserve any less? Over time, self-kindness will feel more automatic, and you'll notice how much happier you feel.

## ASK FOR SUPPORT

Knowing when and how to ask for help may seem like a weakness, but it's actually a strength. After all, everyone encounters difficult situations now and then, and an extra helping hand can make all the difference. Since reaching out for support can feel hard at first, start with something small: Delegate part of a project to a peer or coworker, or ask your partner to help with a chore at home. Then, move up to the bigger things: seeing if an acquaintance will promote your new business, or confiding in a close friend on a difficult day. As you lighten your load or vent about something upsetting, you'll feel the positive effects on your overall happiness—and wonder why you avoided asking for help before.

## ASK THE UNIVERSE FOR HELP

Sometimes things are not within our control—and that's okay! In these instances, a higher power can help lead the way. You just have to ask. First, think about what you want—get specific! Then, write it down, say it out loud, or visualize it as part of your "ask." In this practice, you are manifesting the happiness you want by putting your desires out into the universe, and opening yourself up to whatever comes back.

## DAYDREAM

Letting your mind wander—on your dream job, an innovative idea, or future vacation—leads to more creativity and happiness. In fact, it can actually *improve* productivity, counter to what teachers may have told you! Take some time to sit back and enjoy wherever your thoughts take you.

## AUTOMATE SMALL TASKS

Streamlining small, often repetitive tasks creates valuable space in your day for the things you really enjoy. Consider ordering groceries online, setting up auto-responses for emails, or using media services that consolidate information straight to your fingertips. Then, take a breath and devote that extra time to an activity that makes you happy.

Mindfulness is the ability to recognize what is happening in your mind right now—anger, jealousy, sadness, the pain of a stubbed toe, whatever—without getting carried away by it.

**DAN HARRIS,** author of *10% Happier: How I Tamed the Voice in My Head, Reduced Stress Without Losing My Edge, and Found Self-Help That Actually Works—A True Story*

# PRACTICE MINDFULNESS

Mindfulness is the practice of becoming aware of what is going on around you, as well as what is going on within you (your thoughts and feelings), without passing judgment or trying to change anything. By directing your focus to what is happening, rather than what you think should or might happen, you are pushing the pause button on stress, worry, and any other negative feelings you may have—creating space for happy vibes to take their place.

One easy strategy for practicing mindfulness involves tuning into your five senses. Simply follow these steps:

1 Use your eyes to observe your environment: a tree outside your window, an apple on the kitchen counter, a car parked along the sidewalk you are standing on.
2 Use your ears to notice any sounds occurring: the gentle hum of the radio, the gurgling of the coffee maker, the steady rhythm of your breath.
3 Use your feet or hands to feel your immediate surroundings: your sweatshirt against your skin, the soft carpet underneath your toes.
4 Use your nose to identify different scents: a candle lit in the coffee shop, tomatoes simmering on the stove.
5 Use your tongue to taste any food or drink you are having: buttery toast, sweet lemonade, or just your own mouth.

## ACCEPT A BAD MOOD

We've all been there: You feel yourself sinking into a bad mood and immediately try to convince everyone (and yourself) that you're "fine." And then you end up feeling even more cranky as you fight that uphill battle. Instead, try accepting whatever you're feeling, whether it's sadness, frustration, anxiety, or anger. Say it out loud or write it down, and then practice treating yourself with compassion and a healthy dose of self-care. Maybe you need a good cry, or a transparent conversation, or a change in scenery. Being kind to yourself and accepting that you are feeling a negative emotion—and that it's normal—is a simple way to get yourself on the right track to feeling happy again.

## COMPLETE A VALUE CARDS EXERCISE

A value cards exercise is a great tool to help you identify your values so you can refocus your priorities to manifest those values more in your life. To give it a try, look for a set of premade value cards online or make your own by writing different values on index cards. Check out a list of values online for common ones to include. Next, set a timer for two minutes, and divide the cards into two piles: "important" and "not important." Then set a timer for one minute and pull out your top ten choices from the "important" pile. Now set a timer for thirty seconds and pick your top five from those. These are your top personal values, the things you need to be happy. Brainstorm ways to bring those values into your everyday life; for example, if curiosity is one of your values, carve out time to explore something new.

## GET A PLANT

You probably spend much of your time indoors—even if you're diligent about getting outside on a daily basis. Indoor plants are a great way to bring the revitalizing effects of nature into your home. Put a potted plant on your windowsill, in the corner of the living room, or on your desk at work for a mood boost—and an extra dose of oxygen!

## VENT

Venting every once in a while is surprisingly cathartic for your mood. Instead of faking it if you're feeling down, let it out: Complain out loud, be it to yourself, a friend or family member, or even your pet. Give yourself a solid five minutes to vent, and you'll feel happier for it.

## WRITE YOUR OWN ELEVATOR PITCH

An elevator pitch is a quick, two-to-three-line summary of what makes you stand out as a person or what you're passionate about. It's often used in a work setting, but it's also a great way to remind yourself of why you are awesome—and ensure you are ready for any opportunity to connect with someone new. Brainstorm and then write down your elevator pitch, then practice it with a trusted friend.

## TURN TO YOUR STRENGTHS

Identifying and leveraging the things you do really well—that come naturally to you and feel energizing—helps you to be your best self. It also leads to more happiness, not only because you tend to enjoy the things you have a knack for, but also because that reminder of your strengths is the perfect confidence booster. So make a list of your skills, and put them to use!

## STRIKE UP A CONVERSATION

The ability to talk to anyone may not come naturally to you. Luckily, it's a social skill you can improve with a little practice! Chat up a stranger in line for coffee, or at the next event you attend. It can be extremely rewarding (and fun!) to get to know others, and doing so builds self-confidence—which makes for a happy you.

## DONATE TO A CHARITY

Giving to an organization that does wonderful work in the world not only helps others, but improves your own mood too. After all, doing good feels good! You also have the opportunity to imagine how your donation might make a difference: That ten bucks is a hot meal for someone in need, and that donated coat will keep someone warm during the freezing months.

Being happy isn't having everything in your life be perfect. Maybe it's about stringing together all the little things.

**ANN BRASHARES,**
author of *The Sisterhood of the Traveling Pants*

## EAT A PIECE OF CHOCOLATE

Did you know dark chocolate can be good for your health? It's true: Beyond tasting good, it's pretty much the equivalent of a sweaty workout (well, it mimics the effects, at least!). That's because chocolate contains flavonoids, otherwise known as plant-based antioxidants, which promote better blood flow and help lower cholesterol. Studies have also found that eating chocolate elevates your mood, due to triggering the release of those feel-good endorphins. So treat yourself! Break off a piece of a 70 percent dark chocolate bar, or add a few teaspoons of cocoa to a mug with milk for a rich hot chocolate—and enjoy.

## LIGHT A CANDLE

Candles are more than just easy decorations. That flicker of light creates a cozy, warm ambience that zaps stress and just makes you feel *good* (what were you worried about, again?). There are also different candle scents known for their uplifting qualities, like vanilla, citrus, peppermint, and jasmine. Lighting a favorite candle, seeing it come to life, and letting the warm glow surround you is a simple happiness ritual you can do any time of day. Try a candle with a wooden wick for an added crackling-fire effect reminiscent of snow days spent by the fireplace.

## SNAP A SELFIE

Selfies can get a bad rap, but sometimes taking your own picture makes you feel good about yourself. It's a quick way to boost your self-esteem and appreciate your unique features. Give it a try, and feel free to get a little silly with it—a laugh at your own expense may be just the thing to send a bad mood packing.

## UNSUBSCRIBE FROM JUNK MAIL

Instead of opening your mailbox or email to a bunch of clutter, unsubscribe from all the junk. Check online for easy steps you can take to remove your name from random promotions, coupons, catalogs, etc. Then, unsubscribe from those pesky email newsletters and offers. Now enjoy the freedom of receiving only mail you actually want!

## SAVOR THE FIRST SIP

Mindful drinking, no matter the beverage, allows you to really focus on the present moment and enjoy the smell and taste of whatever is in hand. Maybe it's the sweetness of a lemonade, or the rich warmth of an energizing first sip of coffee in the a.m. Instead of guzzling it down as you run out the door, take a thoughtful sip and enjoy the taste, smell, touch, and even sound of the moment.

## VISIT A THERAPIST

Therapy is a wonderful tool for managing the stress of everyday life, as well as any other obstacles that may get between you and happiness. You'll learn techniques for tackling negative thoughts and emotions head-on; you'll also gain a deeper understanding of yourself and what makes you happy.

## PRACTICE SUN SALUTATIONS

A Sun Salutation is a series of yoga poses done in a sequence to strengthen and tone your muscles. But beyond that, doing Sun Salutations can help release tension and clear negative thoughts. Talk to a yoga teacher or use an online tutorial to learn the poses, then try them at home for a fun mood-booster (and workout!).

## EAT MORE LEAFY GREENS

Leafy, dark greens such as arugula, kale, and spinach are chock-full of natural goodness. They fight inflammation and are high in magnesium, as well as omega-3 fatty acids—both of which improve your mood by relieving symptoms of anxiety and depression. Throw a handful of greens into your omelet, toss them into a homemade soup, or use them in a salad.

## PLAY WITH A MAGNETIC POETRY SET

These sets include hundreds of words in the form of mini magnets that you can mix and match on your refrigerator door. Have fun laying out your favorite song lyrics or making up your own poems to put a smile on your face every time you walk by.

## DRINK A WHEATGRASS SHOT

Wheatgrass has amazing benefits: As a superfood, it packs a punch of vitamins and other nutrients that help promote better health and a happy mood. And because it supports digestion, it can lead to more energy too. Sip on a wheatgrass shot and feel good about nourishing your body.

## PUT ON PAJAMAS

Nothing beats the comfort of slipping into cozy pajamas—especially after a long day. It also serves as a mental transition: You're switching from go-go-go mode to relaxation mode. Knowing the only thing on your agenda is chilling out makes you feel good about the night ahead.

If your happiness depends on
what  somebody else does,
I guess you do have a problem.

**RICHARD BACH,** author of *Illusions:
The Adventures of a Reluctant Messiah*

# BEAT THE COMPARISON TRAP

Ah, the comparison trap: The temptation to compare your life to others'. Thanks to social media, it's easier than ever to scroll through highlight reels of perfect vacations, stylish clothes, and exciting nights out and feel that you don't measure up. And yes, deep down you might know that what people share online is just a small part of the picture: They have their own struggles and less-than-perfect moments. Most people aren't going to post about an argument with family members, or a time they felt insecure. Still, rather than think, "Good for them," you can still find yourself dipping into resentment or envy.

It's not always possible to avoid the comparison trap completely, and that's okay! Instead, focus on how you can get out when you do find yourself swirling into that trap. First, start paying attention to what triggers you to compare yourself, and what causes those FOMO (fear of missing out) feelings. What sort of negative thoughts tend to pop up? Next, remind yourself that it is okay to have these thoughts. Don't beat yourself up for being human! Now, refocus your attention toward living your best life: Think about what's going well, and what skills and awesome qualities you possess. What do you bring to the table that others might not? Take things one step at a time, and after a while it will be easier to kick harmful thoughts to the curb and manifest happiness in their place.

## SMILE

It's one of the oldest tricks in the book: If you're feeling down, smile! Even if it's a bit forced at first, the physical act of smiling sparks a chemical reaction in your brain that increases your sense of happiness. No, really: Studies show that by curling up the corners of your mouth, your brain receives a few doses of dopamine and serotonin, and assumes you're feeling happy—which makes you actually *feel* happier. It's also a lot harder to think negative thoughts when you're smiling. Give it a try, and notice as your bad mood starts to melt away.

## MAKE A BUCKET LIST

Take a few minutes to think about the activities that make you happy, as well as the things you've always wanted to try. Now, make a special "bucket list" of those activities. Remember: This isn't the stuff you think you "should" do—or that you need to do and have put off. This list is for anything that gets you excited about the future. Maybe it includes a day off for yourself, with no plans or obligations. Or you'd like to host a get-together with friends at your place, complete with a massive cheese and crackers board. Or you've been wanting to try the thrill of paragliding. Once you have your list, keep it in a visible spot as a reminder to start checking these items off one by one.

### DRAW WITH CHALK

Grab a set of colored chalk pieces (available at your local dollar store!) and head outside to a paved driveway or sidewalk. Creating colorful words and pictures with chalk is a great way to unwind for a few minutes and tap into a classic childhood joy.

### SCHEDULE LUNCH WITH A PEER

Getting to know someone you typically spend time with in a more formal setting—such as in class or at work—fosters collaboration, leads to productivity, and makes your day-to-day interactions more enjoyable. Suggest a one-to-one outing with someone you're interested in getting to know.

### BOOK A DATE WITH YOURSELF

While it's fun to hang out with friends and significant others, sometimes it's also nice to enjoy something solo. It's a great opportunity to reconnect with yourself and do exactly what makes you happy—without worrying about whether someone else is having fun. Recharge at home or enjoy an afternoon of people-watching at a favorite coffee shop—the time is yours.

### ENJOY SOME GREEN TEA

Green tea is full of antioxidants that fight cancer, protect your DNA, and boost your happiness. In fact, experts say that certain amino acids in green tea reduce feelings of depression and release feel-good chemicals in your body, like dopamine and serotonin. Brew a cup of green tea, sit back, and enjoy the happy vibes.

### TRY A NEW HOBBY

The day-to-day can feel a little monotonous at times, but finding a new hobby helps mix things up and adds an extra dose of excitement to your life. You may even learn something or find new purpose in devoting your time to a meaningful activity. And anything counts! You can take an animation class, learn how to make cheese, or sew your own clothes.

### SEE A CHIROPRACTOR

When your body doesn't feel well, neither does your mind! Visiting a chiropractor can help relieve the standard aches and pains of everyday life, as well as more serious muscle injuries. One adjustment can have you feeling good—inside and out.

# HAPPINESS

is not something you postpone
for the future; it is something
you design for the present.

**JIM ROHN,**
author and entrepreneur

## SAY YES TO A NEW OPPORTUNITY

Taking advantage when a new door opens is a great way to introduce more happiness into your life—especially if you've been feeling a little stuck. You never know what could happen—and that's part of the fun! Maybe going out to a party where you don't know anyone will lead to a new friendship or love connection. Or perhaps signing up for a book club or hobby class on a whim will give drab Wednesday nights a bit more excitement. And as you start saying yes to these opportunities, you'll learn more about yourself and what makes you happy. You'll also push yourself to grow, so you can be the best you possible.

## TAKE A POWER NAP

We all love the joy of a leisurely three-hour nap—but research shows that taking a twenty- to thirty-minute power nap is better for your health. It helps you catch up on Zs without making it harder to fall asleep that night. It also improves your mood and energy levels, allowing you to be more productive and focused later on. Think of it like a free mini vacation in the middle of the day!

## POP BUBBLE WRAP

There's a certain satisfaction to popping the bubbles in bubble wrap, and researchers agree. The pressure and release, and the finger and hand movements involved, help reduce stress and draw your attention away from negative thoughts or emotions. Hang onto the bubble wrap when you get a package so you can pull it out whenever crabby feelings hit and pop your way to a happy mood!

## MAKE YOUR BED

Making your bed creates a sense of accomplishment, which can kick-start your day and keep you on a productive path. The way your room looks also impacts your mood, so a tidy bed helps you feel more relaxed and positive. Use clean sheets fresh from the dryer for a boost.

## ENJOY A GREEN JUICE

Green juice is full of antioxidants that give your physical *and* mental health a boost. You'll feel proud of yourself for adding an extra dose of nutrients and energy to your day. Plus, there are tons of delicious combinations of fruits and veggies you can try. If you're making your own version at home, use a ratio of two veggies per one fruit.

If you want happiness for an hour,
take a nap. If you want happiness for
a day, go fishing. If you want happiness
for a month, get married. If you want
happiness for a year, inherit a fortune.
If you want happiness for a lifetime,
help somebody else.

Chinese proverb

# OFFER A HELPING HAND

Remember the last time someone helped you? It's a great feeling, right? When your roommate picks up your favorite box of cereal at the grocery store, a stranger gives you a coupon code for an online store, your significant other washes your car—it feels beyond comforting to be cared for. And when you're the one offering a helping hand, it feels just as good—if not more so.

Research even backs it up: Psychologists reason that participating in acts of kindness releases endorphins in your brain, similar to when you're pushing through the end of an intense workout. Ever heard of a "runner's high"? It's kind of the same thing, known as a "helper's high." Helping people makes you feel happier, especially when you're able to align the way you're helping with your values and relationships. For example, hold the door for the person behind you in line. Help your older family member set up a social media account. Ask your friends if they need support in anything right now. Be the person who brings donuts to work on a random Monday, or offers to mow the lawn for your neighbors.

## TALK TO YOUR NEIGHBOR

Before you give the usual quick wave to your neighbor and continue speed-walking to your car, consider stopping for a short chat instead. Research suggests being neighborly creates a sense of connection, builds trust, and leads to happy, more engaged communities. It also makes where you live feel more homey. So get to know some of the people who live near you. Ask questions, drop off a loaf of banana bread as a kind gesture, or invite them over for a game night. Over time, you may even offer to help them out by walking their dog or keeping an eye on their place when they're out of town. (Bonus: They'll probably return the favor the next time you need a hand!)

## CHECK SOMETHING OFF YOUR TO-DO LIST

Unsurprisingly, productivity leads to happiness: Checking items off your to-do list is incredibly satisfying and makes you feel accomplished. Plus, the more you can cross things off a list, the more motivation you'll have to keep going. Spend some time making your list if you haven't already, then check something off! One tip: Remember to include smaller tasks on your list that move you closer to your larger goals. For example, if setting up a blog has been a dream since forever, break it into smaller to-dos, like creating a list of potential blog names and mapping out the content you want to include.

### EMBRACE OPPOSING FEELINGS

Our emotions aren't always black and white, either/or feelings we can clearly label or put into boxes. Sometimes they can even contradict each other. But no worries—it's normal! You can be annoyed with your sibling and love her deeply; you can feel excited about a new opportunity and also terrified. Accepting the whole spectrum of your emotions—rather than spiraling into even more complex emotions of guilt and disappointment with yourself—is a huge part of finding real happiness in this crazy world.

### JOIN A ZUMBA CLASS

Zumba is a unique style of exercise inspired by Latin America's dance traditions. This fun, full-body workout not only burns calories, but also improves your cardio endurance over time and signals the release of "happy hormones" like serotonin. Zumba can be enjoyed in a group class or at home with online videos, and the intensity can be dialed up or down depending on your fitness level.

### MASTER A NEW SKILL

Learning something new, whether it's a language, an unfamiliar subject, a sport, or something else, truly makes your brain smarter and stronger. It also boosts self-confidence and promotes continued curiosity in new things. Pick something to explore and have fun pushing yourself out of your comfort zone!

## PET A FURRY FRIEND

If you have a pet at home, then you already know: Pets bring so much happiness into our lives, in all sorts of ways. First, scratching a dog's scruff or petting a cat's furry back feels good to the touch, especially when you get a tail wag or purr as a seal of approval. Second, all that playing fetch and walking (or leading them around the house with a string) improves blood pressure, decreases your risk of heart disease, and releases feel-good endorphins. Finally, just being around a pet has a calming effect; consider it pet therapy!

## MASTER A CARD GAME

Anytime you feel accomplished, it puts a little spring in your step. So when you're looking for a quick mood boost, practice your skills in a popular card game. You can master a game you've never played before, or build on skills you already have in a favorite game. If you are a beginner, start by checking out online tutorials, or having an experienced friend or family member show you the ropes. And if you want to work on current skills, invite some friends over for a little friendly competition. With a big group, try spoons. Only two players? Give cribbage a go. No matter what you choose to master, lay your cards on the table and enjoy the thrill of the game.

## MEMORIZE THE LYRICS TO A SONG

You're in the car and one of your all-time favorite songs comes on—what do you do? Start belting out the lyrics, of course! Nothing beats knowing every single word to a great tune, and this type of memorization is really good for your brain too. And because singing releases endorphins and brings more oxygen into your blood, it's the perfect quick pick-me-up whenever you're feeling down.

## VISIT A BODY OF WATER

If you've ever been to an ocean or looked out onto a river or lake, you know how peaceful being near water can feel. Looking at the water as it moves and hearing its sounds—from waves crashing against the shore to the idyllic trickling of a waterfall—has an uplifting effect on your mood.

## MAKE A PHOTO BOOK

There's something heartwarming about being able to see, hold, and touch pictures of special moments IRL. Check out an online service that does the work for you with fun templates, and build a book of memories to flip through every time you need a lift.

## USE A SLEEP MASK

The darker your room, the better you sleep—and the more rested and fresh you feel in the morning. Try wearing a sleep mask to block out everything from moonlight to the LED light on your alarm clock so you can doze in peace.

## POUR A DRINK IN A FANCY GLASS

Don't save that fancy glass for a special occasion: Bust it out at any time for whatever beverage you choose. There's something about pouring your usual water into a tall goblet, or using a champagne flute for your morning orange juice, that feels special and brings a little festivity into play as you quench your thirst.

## TAKE A HOT SHOWER

A warm, steamy shower is relaxing and uplifting. It helps you wake up in the morning and rinse off the day before bed. And if you're not feeling well, whether mentally or physically, a hot shower can provide a nice reset. Enjoy the cozy temperature, and make sure to moisturize afterward for additional pampering: You deserve it!

There's nothing like deep breaths after laughing that hard. Nothing in the world like a sore stomach for the right reasons.

**STEPHEN CHBOSKY,**
author of *The Perks of Being a Wallflower*

## WATCH THE SUN RISE

Happiness can come from the smallest moments: Waking up early to watch the sun rise is one of them. It will be worth it to grab a cup of coffee and gaze out the window (or step outside!) to watch the new day begin in a gorgeous array of colors.

## READ A COMIC

If you traditionally pick up fiction or nonfiction books, try reading comics or graphic novels. It'll help you appreciate visual storytelling, and you'll be more likely to stay super present while reading, since you'll be taking in the art and text of each page closely. Comics are a simple, uplifting way to step into a new world and let imagination take the lead.

## JUMP ROPE

When's the last time you jumped rope? Probably as a kid, right? It's time to bring back this classic that is guaranteed to boost your mood! Pick up a cheap rope from a sporting goods store or order one online. You'll feel lighter on your feet, get a heart-pumping workout in, and have fun revitalizing a childhood pastime.

## DRESS UP

When you look good, you feel good. Instead of throwing on your usual sweats, put on a confidence-boosting dress, power suit, or chic skirt-blouse combo. You can dress up for a date out with friends or a significant other, or a day in with yourself.

## MAKE AN ENERGY-EFFICIENT SWITCH

A simple swap to compact fluorescent light bulbs is better for your budget, the environment—*and* your mood. You'll feel good knowing you're doing your part to reduce how much energy you use at home (and make your appliances and electronics last longer).

## REPAINT A ROOM

The color of a room dramatically impacts your mood. Some colors appeal to you simply because of personal preference, while others are proven to have certain effects: Blue promotes calm and productivity, whereas red inspires strong emotions (and an appetite). If you've got a space where the color isn't quite working for you, grab a paintbrush and freshen things up! Not only is painting a fun activity, but you'll also end up with a room that brings you joy every time you step through the door.

All of us who do creative work...we get into it because we have good taste. But there is a gap. For the first couple years that you're making stuff, what you're making isn't so good....It's trying to be good, it has ambition to be good, but it's not quite that good. But your taste, the thing that got you into the game, your taste is still killer. And your taste is good enough that you can tell that what you're making is kind of a disappointment to you....Everybody goes through that. If you're going through it right now, or if you're just getting out of that phase, you gotta know it's totally normal....It is only by actually going through a volume of work that you're actually going to catch up and close that gap, and the work you're making will be as good as your ambitions.

**IRA GLASS,** host and producer of *This American Life*

# TAP INTO YOUR CREATIVITY

Studies suggest that creative activities spark something called an "upward spiral" of emotion and well-being—in other words, happiness. And you don't have to be a paid artist or work in a creative field: Anyone who likes to play an instrument, sketch or doodle, or create DIY crafts can benefit from making time for regular creativity. Maybe you like to make inspiration boards on *Pinterest*, or write corny song lyrics, or design colorful Excel spreadsheets: It all counts! Anything that encourages you to think outside of the box, come up with original ideas, make connections between concepts, and problem-solve is a creative activity. The result? Less anxiety, more resilience, and a stronger sense of playfulness—all of which factor into your overall happiness.

One thing to keep in mind: This is about being creative, not building a masterpiece. Remember to have fun as you create, and don't get caught up in whether the result is perfect. Besides, it's practice that will get you to that masterpiece (if that is the goal).

## SWAP CLOTHES WITH A FRIEND

You sift through your closet and think about how you have "nothing" to wear. Instead of heading out the door to buy something new, or filling up your online cart, try setting up a clothes swap with friends. Have everyone bring the clothes they never wear anymore, or that no longer fit, and have some fun trading them. Your gently used clothes will get a second life, and you'll walk away a happier (and more stylish) version of yourself. You'll also save money, which always feels good, and make a more sustainable choice for the planet.

## CANCEL PLANS

Despite how much you may love getting together with friends or visiting a close family member, sometimes you want nothing more than to cancel all your plans in favor of chilling alone on the couch or going to bed early. And that's okay! It's actually better for your happiness to bail on plans once in a while, instead of forcing yourself to do something you don't feel up for. Be honest about what you need, offer to reschedule, and then cut yourself some slack.

## BUILD A SOUNDING BOARD

When you're trying to solve a problem, you might be too close to the issue to see it clearly. And that's where having a sounding board of trusted family members and/or friends can be super helpful. Ask for their insights into a situation, or ask them to just hear you out as you vent about what's bothering you. You'll feel supported, and you'll likely end up with more clarity too.

## TRY AN ABHYANGA MASSAGE

This self-massage comes from Ayurveda, an ancient healing system from India. With Abhyanga, you use a warm, herb-infused oil to massage your body from head to toe, in a wonderful act of love and appreciation for yourself. (It can also help calm nerves, aid in detoxing and circulation, and more!)

## MAKE AN INDULGENT HOT CHOCOLATE

When you're feeling a little down in the dumps, a warm cup of delicious hot chocolate can be just the thing to lift your mood (and bring you back to fond childhood memories). Get a little fancy by topping it with whipped cream and shaved chocolate.

## THINK A HAPPY THOUGHT

It might sound too simple, but thinking positive thoughts really does make you feel happier. When you're feeling down in the dumps, or notice any negative thoughts creeping in, think something positive: "The weather is so nice today" or "I am a great listener." Repeat the thought in your head (or out loud!) and feel the good vibes take over.

## JOURNAL ABOUT YOUR DAY

Jotting down your daily observations—the small things that made you happy, creative ideas, little moments of joy—helps build your self-esteem and reminds you to relish each day. Journaling also teaches you to be mindful: You can work through any current anxieties or frustrations and process how you're feeling, so you can let go of the things that get between you and happiness.

## PRACTICE BODY NEUTRALITY

Body neutrality is when you accept your body for what it looks and feels like now. You aren't forcing yourself to love or even like what you see in the mirror, and you're not disliking it, either (a feeling that affects the happiness of a lot of people). To practice this, look at yourself in the mirror and say an affirmation like, "I am okay with how my body looks and feels today."

If you are depressed, you are living in the past.
If you are anxious, you are living in the future.
If you are at peace, you are living in the present.

———

**Unknown**

## IDENTIFY WHAT'S ANNOYING YOU

The moment you feel annoyed or frustrated by something, you might shut down ("Whatever, this isn't a big deal") or lash out ("Ugh! Why does this always happen to me?"). However, there's a simple alternative that'll help you let go of that negative feeling and create space for happiness in its place: Sit with the feeling for a few minutes. Explore what's really bugging you and why. Maybe that argument you had last week with your friend is still lingering like a dark cloud over your mood, or you're secretly nervous about an upcoming interview. Once you tap into the "why," you can then focus on solving the problem versus ruminating (and eventually exploding) over a bad mood.

## FIND YOUR GO-TO MANTRA

A mantra is a particular word or phrase recited to manifest positive thoughts and emotions, and quiet any negative chatter in your brain. You can find different mantras online to try out, or come up with your own. To create your own, think about what you want to focus on; it might be the concept of "happiness," or a full sentence, like "I am welcoming happiness into my life." Once you land on your mantra, add it into your daily routine: Whisper it to yourself over your morning cup of coffee, or say it in your head a few times before bed. As you recite your mantra, you'll notice happy vibes starting to manifest.

## DO AN AT-HOME FACIAL

An at-home facial is the perfect (and inexpensive) way to treat yourself. Wash your face thoroughly, use a gentle exfoliator to remove dead skin cells, then wipe with an alcohol-free toner. Your skin will feel happy too!

## GO SHOPPING

It's called retail therapy for a reason: Buying something new, whether to cheer yourself up or in celebration of an accomplishment, helps reduce anxiety and makes you feel good about your life. Shopping also encourages you to visualize what comes next as part of your best self or best life. It's fun, and you get something new for your wardrobe.

## POP A CBD GUMMY

Cannabidiol, otherwise known as CBD, is a natural remedy for chronic pain, insomnia, anxiety, and symptoms of depression. Although it is one of the chemicals found in the cannabis plant, CBD doesn't impact your psychological state. Look for a reputable brand, and enjoy a CBD gummy whenever you need a little boost. (Just be sure to check in with your doctor first.)

I used to fear hearing the term, "Who do you think you are?" or "You must be pretty full of yourself..." Now, I work at being full. I want to be so full, I am overflowing...with enough to share with everybody else. I'm going to own the fullness without ego, without arrogance, but with an amazing sense of gratitude.

**OPRAH WINFREY,** media executive

# BE (A LITTLE) FULL OF YOURSELF

Confidence matters! When you know who you are and what you want, you carry yourself with courage, determination, and integrity. You trust your feelings, opinions, and decisions, because you believe in your intentions, judgment, and ability to keep moving forward. Most importantly, you see your own worth and accept that you deserve happiness. You are "full of yourself" in all the right ways.

So, how do you become more like Oprah? Start by embracing your own worthiness: Make a list of what you're good at, recent wins where your strengths really shined, and any challenging situations that you managed to resolve. Now give yourself a hand for how awesome you are! Keep this list in a place where you can reread it anytime self-doubt creeps in. Revisit it whenever you feel yourself worrying more about getting praise (and receiving attention or rewards from others) than about whether *you* feel proud about what you are doing.

## READ A NOVEL

Reading anything is good for your brain—a fun whodunit, the biography or memoir of a pop icon, or a collection of essays all challenge your memory and improve critical thinking. But picking up a novel specifically gives you a little break from facts in favor of exercising your imagination. Following fictional characters opens your mind to unique perspectives and encourages you to think outside the box. It also reduces stress by redirecting your focus, and leads to better sleep. Plus, it's just fun! Think of it as a way to travel to new worlds—without spending a dime.

## SET UP A "HAPPY FUND"

When you think about saving money, you probably zero in on the necessities: an emergency fund, a down payment on a new car, paying off loans, etc. And those are important expenses. However, not all your money needs to be untouchable! A little bit of discretionary spending can lift your spirits and give you something to look forward to. Start setting your spare dollars aside in a dedicated "fun money" fund, where you can budget for the things that make you happy. This fund can be put toward little pleasures like a delicious latte on a chaotic Monday morning, and/ or bigger items like tickets to see your favorite band.

## NOTE WHAT'S GOING WELL

We are all wired to pick up on anything that goes wrong. It's not our fault! However, when you do find yourself going down that path, you can beat out negative thoughts by refocusing on the things that are going well. Recognize the ways life is good, and you'll feel good.

## WATCH A CARTOON

Throw back to your childhood by enjoying a beloved cartoon you haven't seen in ages. When you're feeling stressed or a bit down in the dumps, cartoons are an easy way to lift your mood and release your worries. Animated films also do the trick!

## TAKE A $B_{12}$ SUPPLEMENT

Low $B_{12}$ levels are a common problem that can leave you feeling down. Consider adding a daily $B_{12}$ supplement to your diet to improve your mood. Increasing your $B_{12}$ levels will also strengthen your memory and prevent fatigue.

In every moment of every day,

we get to choose whom we listen to:

**WORRY** or **WONDER**.

**AMBER RAE,**
author of *Choose Wonder Over Worry:*
*Move Beyond Fear and Doubt to Unlock Your Full Potential*

# MAKE TIME FOR WONDER

One common obstacle to happiness is uncertainty. It causes feelings of stress and fear, as you agonize over what is going to happen. When uncertainty starts threatening your mood, imagine that you have two voices in your head: one that gently nudges you to view the world with a sense of curiosity and wonder, and another that constantly worries about everything that could go wrong. Curiosity serves as a driving force for creativity, satisfaction, and even your health. Research links it to both a better mood and improved self-esteem. Meanwhile, that worry about negative possibilities may seem like it's trying to protect you, but know that even good intentions can be harmful. It's time to start listening to your voice of wonder. Give the thrill of novelty and new experiences the floor!

When you're thinking about the future and start fretting about what might happen, pivot: What great possibilities could be in store? What might you discover? Letting curiosity lead helps you find happiness throughout the ups and downs of life.

## GRAB A HANDFUL OF WALNUTS

Walnuts often get overlooked for the classic favorite, peanuts, or "fancier" almonds. But it's time to give this superfood the attention it deserves! Walnuts are a major source of omega-3 fats, which fight stress and lower your blood pressure. Studies also show walnuts promote tryptophan, an amino acid that produces serotonin, the feel-good chemical that is key to happiness, improved energy levels, and healthy sleep habits. Throw a handful of walnuts into your salad, add them to a sweet-and-salty trail mix, or enjoy them alone for a tasty treat that makes you smile.

## STRETCH FROM SIDE TO SIDE

While most people reserve stretching for a pre-run warm-up or casual yoga class, it is actually a great way to improve your mood at any time. Stretching releases endorphins, those same exhilarating hormones that make you feel great after a hard workout. Consider adding it to your daily routine. Touching your toes and reaching your arms high above your head are easy go-to moves, but you can also stretch from side to side to improve posture and circulation as well. Whether you're sitting or standing, send your hands up toward the sky, then lean over to the right, and then to the left. As you stretch, pull your tummy in, and keep your spine straight and your chin pointed forward for alignment. You can also clasp your hands together above your head.

## WEAR A HAPPY COLOR

Did you know wearing certain colors can make you feel happy? Warm colors like orange, red, and yellow represent happy energy, and cooler colors such as purple, green, and blue can be soothing. You can mix and match your clothing depending on how different shades impact your mood, and pick new clothes that you feel good in.

## DO A ONE-MINUTE WALL SIT

You probably already know that it's better for both your mood and your health to be more active, but it can be tricky to work in activity if most of your day involves sitting at a desk. Enter the wall sit: It's an easy exercise you can do anywhere, anytime. To do a wall sit, lean your back against a wall with your knees bent at a ninety-degree angle and your feet planted flat on the floor. Hold the position for a minute, then rest and repeat two more times. Try doing this a few times throughout the day.

## MAXIMIZE YOUR COMMUTE

If you travel back and forth regularly for a job or class, you know the daily commute can have a real impact on your mood. Maximize this time by spending it in a way that makes you happier. Listen to a new playlist or podcast while biking or driving. Read a good book or watch funny videos if you take a train or bus. Don't let this time go to waste!

### CLOSE YOUR COMPUTER

Unplugging every once in a while does wonders for your mood: You pull yourself out of "reactive" mode and give your brain a break from the nonstop stream of information. It also creates more time for doing something fun in order to recharge: spending time with friends or family, exercising, enjoying a favorite hobby, and more. Less FOMO, more JOMO.

### LEARN A NEW DANCE

Moving your body is a fun way to release feel-good hormones—and get a mini workout in in the process. Learning a new type of dance, whether by taking a class or watching how-to videos at home, will have you feeling happy and confident— especially when you nail the moves! From salsa to swing dancing to hip-hop or the tango, any dance will do the trick.

### STYLE A SHELF

You don't have to be an interior designer to spruce up a shelf at home. Start by clearing off any clutter, then think about what you'd like to showcase: a couple of beautiful books, a vintage brass figurine, a small piece of art, favorite photos, and more. It'll make your space feel homier, and highlight some of your most beloved items—giving your mood a little boost every time you see it.

But to be happy it is essential not to be too concerned with others.

**ALBERT CAMUS,** philosopher

One cannot think well,

love well,

sleep well,

if one has not dined well.

**VIRGINIA WOOLF,**
author of *A Room of One's Own*

# COOK A YUMMY MEAL

Cooking can be an amazing way to reduce stress and improve your mood. In fact, experts say people feel more positive after eating at home and tend to choose healthier meals later on as well. You can zone out chopping, measuring, and combining ingredients—or turn it into a fun game, pretending you are in a cooking competition or on a cooking show.

Throughout the process, you'll have the chance to get creative, build confidence (as you figure out how to make your dish and troubleshoot any problems), and then enjoy a sense of accomplishment as you nourish yourself—and maybe your friends and family too! Cooking also promotes mindfulness, helping you tune into your senses: the smell of the roasting veggies, the feel of the dough as you knead it for a pizza crust, the taste of chili straight from the pot. So the next time you need a little boost, turn on some music and start cooking!

## WASH THE DISHES

Okay, hear us out: Yes, washing the dishes is a chore, but it's also one that can lower your stress level and help you tune into the present, leading to more happiness. Instead of racing to get every plate, cup, and bowl into the dishwasher or grumbling as you scrub your way through pots and pans, consider the activity a way to decompress and practice mindfulness. When using the sink, focus your attention on the details: the smell of the soap you're using, the heat of the water, the clink of the spoons. Think about the act of cleaning the dishes—how satisfying it is to turn a tower of messy plates cluttering the sink or counter into a squeaky-clean row on the drying rack. Finding even a little joy in an everyday chore is definitely something to feel happy about.

## START A TRADITION

Whether with family members, friends, a significant other, or yourself, a new tradition can add a dose of excitement to your life. Maybe you decide to bake a cake on your half-birthday every year, or light sparklers on the first official day of summer. It'll give you something to look forward to in addition to the usual holidays and events!

## TELL SOMEONE YOU LOVE THEM

Saying "I love you" to someone you care about—the BFF you've known forever, a close family member, or the love of your life—feels good. Plus, people deserve to know they are special to you! Telling someone you love them has a positive effect on everyone involved.

## LAUGH AT YOURSELF

Whether you're cracking a self-deprecating joke or chuckling at yourself for tripping up the stairs, remembering to laugh at yourself is key when it comes to a healthy, happy you. Experts note that this ability improves emotional well-being and boosts resiliency, making you better able to cope with stress and tackle anything that comes your way.

## ENTER A CONTEST

If you've ever bought a lottery ticket or entered your email address for a chance to win a getaway vacation, you understand the happy thrill of betting your odds for a worthwhile prize. It's just plain fun to try to win something! So try different types of contests—magazine sweepstakes, social media photo competitions, trivia night at a local restaurant—and ride the high of possibility.

Happiness can be found,

even in the darkest of times,

if one only remembers

to **TURN ON THE LIGHT.**

**J.K. ROWLING,**
author of *Harry Potter and the Prisoner of Azkaban*

# FIND THE SILVER LINING

As a human, you're biologically programmed to react to danger with an increased heart rate and rush of adrenaline. But nowadays, even when the biggest "threat" is a pending deadline or changing traffic light, your body can still default to high alert, which wreaks havoc on your happiness over time. To combat this reaction, seek out the silver lining in a negative situation. Of course, looking on the bright side can feel easier said than done—however, with practice, you can train your brain to think positively by default.

Start by identifying when you are having a negative thought or feeling. Accept that it is there, and ask yourself, "Is there another angle to this?" Maybe you've been stressing about a relationship, focusing on what you feel is going wrong. What positives could come from this rough patch? Maybe you will learn better ways to communicate with the other person so they can fully understand your thoughts and feelings—and you can understand theirs. Struggling to find income lately? Maybe this time can teach you more about self-sufficiency and staying confident in a difficult situation. Dealing with an illness? Maybe you'll find a new appreciation for your body and what it's capable of when healthy. There is always another perspective, so take a second look from a different angle.

### MAKE IMPROMPTU PLANS

There's nothing worse than dreading plans scheduled in advance. Even if they were made with your closest pals, sometimes that day rolls around and you just wish you could cancel, or hope they do. Hey, things happen: Life gets stressful, you have an off day, or you just aren't feeling it like you were when the plans were made. Instead, try seizing those times when you *are* feeling it: Make a spontaneous coffee date, or go for an impromptu walk together. Enjoy yourself—unforced.

### WEAR FUZZY SOCKS

A great pair of socks makes all the difference. Think about pulling on extra-cozy, warm socks in your favorite color or pattern—hard not to smile, right? They are such an easy way to bring more comfort and relaxation wherever you go. Treat yourself to an ultra-plush pair with a fun design that makes you happy every time you look at them.

### WRITE WITH A BRAND-NEW PEN

Finding the right pen to suit your preference—ballpoint, rollerball, gel, Sharpie, fountain—is a very specific kind of joy. It has to have the right grip, ink that writes well, the durability to withstand being tossed into your bag, and a price that doesn't break the bank. Once you land on a favorite, enjoy the small delight of writing with your brand-new pen.

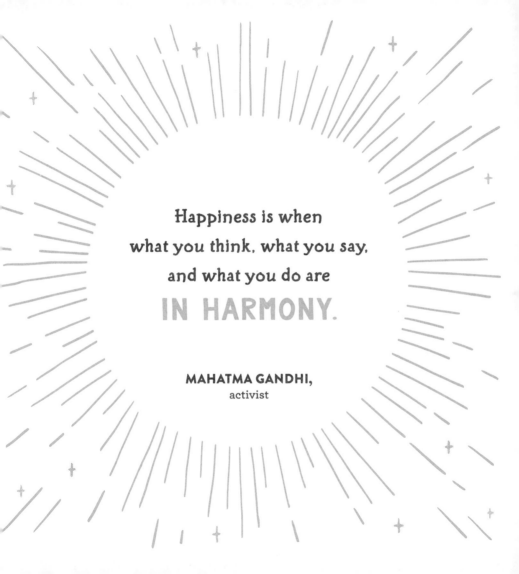

Happiness is when
what you think, what you say,
and what you do are

# IN HARMONY.

**MAHATMA GANDHI,**
activist

## SMOOTH SHEA BUTTER LOTION ON YOUR HANDS

Shea butter lotion—a hydrating, thick, all-natural cream full of vitamins, healthy fatty acids, and anti-inflammatories—feels luxurious on your skin. It's also multi-purpose; you can use it on your arms and legs, as well as your face, to soothe and moisturize dry skin and keep you feeling soft. Dab a little shea butter lotion into your hands and take a few moments to mindfully smooth it over your palms and each finger until your skin feels silky-smooth. It's a simple way to include a little self-care in your daily routine: Happy skin, happy you!

## WEAR YOUR FAVORITE OUTFIT

When you look your best, you feel your best, so the saying goes. And it's true! What you wear influences your mood: A sharp blazer can make you feel like a boss, while those thread-bare sweatpants from five years ago make you feel, well, not quite as ready to take on the day. Think about which outfits or specific articles of clothing in your closet make you feel happiest. There's no wrong answer. Wearing your favorite pieces will give you an extra boost whenever you need it.

## GET A HAIRCUT

Your hair absolutely impacts your mood—and how you feel about yourself. When you're feeling a little off, schedule a haircut (or even just a shampoo and trim) for a fresh look, as well as a fresh outlook on life. It will give you a dose of self-confidence and something to show off to friends and family members.

## BAKE A DESSERT

From chocolatey cupcakes to peanut butter cookies to blueberry muffins, there's something special about making—and eating!—a delicious dessert or baked good. The act of baking also requires your full attention, making it easier to send any stressed feelings or negative thoughts packing. And that first bite? Yum. Go ahead and indulge.

## WAKE UP EARLY

Early bird gets the worm, and experts say morning people are also happier. For one thing, if you're waking up early, you're more likely to go to bed on time and get a good night's sleep. For another, that early alarm clock can mean a little time for self-care before you have to head out the door. You can use your time to read or exercise, or just make your morning routine a bit less hectic.

## ORGANIZE YOUR JUNK DRAWER

Everybody has a junk drawer full of random stuff—hot sauce packets, coupons, rubber bands, pens. But when you actually need one of those items, it's hard to find in all the clutter. Organizing this drawer—or any messy drawer in your home—is an easy way to clear your head and feel productive. Plus, it's liberating to toss out what you don't need!

## SAY "I'LL THINK ABOUT IT"

Whenever confronted with a question or request, remember that you don't have to respond with a yes or no right away. Instead, you can say, "I'll think about it," which buys you a little time to reflect and gather more information before making a decision. It also creates some space for you to honor whatever feelings may pop up, allowing you to follow up in a more authentic way. This easy practice in authenticity is a great way to cultivate more long-term happiness.

## LOOK AT THE STARS

Stargazing is a fun, simple activity to do either alone or with a loved one. It's also a great way to get a new perspective: The planets, constellations, and our massive galaxy are so much bigger than anything that might be weighing you down! Plus, seeing the beauty of the dark skies above sparks reflection, observation, and contemplation. You can think about your place in the universe—or look for the Big Dipper.

Very little is needed to make a happy life.

Unknown

Mindset change is not about picking up a few pointers here and there. It's about seeing things in a new way. When people—couples, coaches and athletes, managers and workers, parents and children, teachers and students— change to a growth mindset, they change from a judge-and-be-judged framework to a learn-and-help-learn framework. Their commitment is to growth, and growth takes plenty of time, effort, and mutual support.

**CAROL DWECK,** psychologist and author of *Mindset: The New Psychology of Success*

# MAINTAIN A GROWTH MINDSET

In the face of challenge, consider how you react. Do you feel curious about trying to solve the problem? Or do you immediately go into a panicked, this-will-never-work mode? Psychologist Carol Dweck calls this a "growth" mindset versus a "fixed" mindset. A "fixed" mindset views creativity, character, and intellect as static and innate; success is the by-product of how skilled or smart you are, and you can't do anything to change that. Conversely, a "growth" mindset sees challenges as an opportunity for growth across those same categories; failure doesn't mean you aren't skilled or smart, just that you're stretching yourself and may or may not succeed in doing so. There is possibility for improvement.

Nurturing a "growth" mindset is an important part of becoming the best, happiest you that you can be. To develop your "growth" mindset muscles, start by appreciating your effort: the time you put into a thank-you note for a friend, how you worked to polish your speech in private before that big presentation. Focus less on perfection or outcomes, and more on the process. As you get better at appreciating your effort, you can also start reflecting on your mistakes, exploring what can be done differently next time, and what lessons you can take away from the experience. Seek out feedback from others if you choose, and look forward to trying again in the future. Setbacks are normal: It's what you do with them that makes the difference!

## TRY LIGHT THERAPY

If you live in a region where certain times of year bring constant cold and/or darkness, you can be at risk for seasonal affective disorder (known as SAD). Seasonal affective disorder is a common problem in which your mood is negatively impacted by the changing seasons. You may notice symptoms of depression creeping in as the weather gets colder and the days get shorter. Luckily, you can beat the seasonal blues with light therapy! A light therapy device mimics natural light, minimizing moodiness and increasing your energy level. Check out different options online to find one that fits your living space.

## ASK A NEW FRIEND TO HANG OUT

Okay, so you just met an awesome new acquaintance, someone you can see yourself being friends with—now what? Get that ball rolling by asking them to hang out! You can make your invitation low-stakes: "I'm going to check out that bookstore down the street later on; want to join me?" You'll feel proud of putting yourself out there and may even make a new best friend in the process.

## DRINK COFFEE

Sipped in moderation, coffee wards off feelings of stress and anxiety. Caffeine stimulates the release of dopamine, making you feel positive and amped up for the day ahead. So drink a cup or two (before 5 p.m. for the best results) for an instant mood boost.

## INDULGE IN AN ICE CREAM CONE

When's the last time you ate a sugar cone topped with a scoop (or three) of your favorite ice cream, or a waffle cone piled with rich frozen custard? Whether it's been months or days, take some time to indulge. This old-fashioned dessert inspires memories of childhood ice cream treats, like the jingle of the ice cream truck coming down the street. You can't help but feel happy!

## ENJOY A BELLY LAUGH

A big belly laugh changes your mood in an instant. For starters, it shrinks stress hormones and lowers blood pressure; it also provides a much-needed distraction. You can't stay in a foul mood when you're doubled over laughing with friends at a hilarious story. And if you're solo, just watch funny videos or a comedy to get the laughs going.

## PUT YOUR COINS IN A JAR

Every little bit of change saved adds up. And seeing coins pile up in a jar can provide a jolt of confidence around other financial goals. If you don't typically carry cash, try digital tools that automate the process; some apps will round up every purchase and put the extra change into a separate savings account. The result? Extra money to spend on whatever makes you happy.

## CALL OR TEXT SOMEONE

Every year, it seems more of the people you know are moving to different places, or just leading busier and busier lives that make getting together that much harder. However, a big part of happiness comes from nurturing the positive relationships you have—no matter distance or schedules. Make a point of giving your friends a quick call or sending at least semi-regular texts to keep your connection strong. Not only will it allow you to remain a consistent part of their lives, but it will also encourage them to reach out more regularly too. It's fulfilling to have reminders that your friends are there for you (and vice versa), and those small moments—receiving an emoji that makes you smile, reminiscing about that summer trip during high school, or catching up for ten minutes during your morning commute—go a long way.

## VOLUNTEER AT AN ANIMAL RESCUE

When you're feeling low, an easy way to flip your mood is by helping a furry friend in need. Look into opportunities to volunteer at a local animal shelter, whether it's walking dogs, playing with kittens, or getting the word out about adoption. There is no shortage of ways you can help out, and it feels so good when you do. Not only that, but you get to spend time petting and playing with adorable dogs, cats, bunnies, and more—what's better than that? And if you want to learn more ways you can help, just check out information online. From donations to petitions, there are tons of ways to make a difference for animals around the world.

### ENJOY SOME JUICY BERRIES

Blueberries, strawberries, raspberries, blackberries—any of these delicious berries pack an antioxidant-rich punch. They help manage free radicals (oxygen-containing molecules that can lead to cell damage if they get too high in number) in your body. Better yet, they can prevent the release of cortisol, a hormone linked to stress. Snack your way to healthy and happy!

### VACUUM

Vacuuming is one of those daily chores (okay, weekly...or monthly) that you may dread at first but which ends up feeling oh-so-satisfying once you're done. Your floors look much cleaner and your home feels cozier and less cluttered. Out with the dirt and dust; in with the fresh, reinvigorating atmosphere!

### DO A HAIR MASK

Hair treatment masks add moisture to your locks, minimize frizz, and help protect your scalp. Plus, they are a luxe way to pamper yourself anytime. You can buy a hair mask at the store, or experiment with a DIY version. If you decide to go DIY, choose nourishing ingredients like honey, eggs, bananas, and olive or coconut oil. When your hair looks and feels good, so do you.

Burnout often has as much
boredom in it as exhaustion.

**INGRID FETELL LEE,**
author of *Joyful: The Surprising Power of Ordinary
Things to Create Extraordinary Happiness*

# TAKE A REST

You've probably been taught to devote as much of your energy toward being productive as possible, but you aren't a machine, you're a person—who needs downtime. Think of a computer: If you open up every single program and application and never hit the off button, it's going to crash at some point. People are the same way; we need periods of rest in order to reset our minds and avoid the burnouts that lead to forgetfulness, exhaustion, and feeling unhappy. Plus, giving your brain a chance to press pause will actually help you be more successful later. It's like when you have a brilliant idea in the shower after feeling stuck the entire previous day. Sometimes that break is just what you needed to see the problem or task from a new angle.

So stop working: Put down your phone, shut that computer, and skip the chores. Avoid picking up a book or turning on the TV too. Yes—we are giving you full permission to do absolutely nothing. It's up to you whether you take a break for a few minutes or a few hours; just listen to what your mind and body need. You'll feel recharged, upbeat, and ready to take on anything that comes your way!

## SEND A "YOU'RE AWESOME" NOTE

You're familiar with sending thank-you cards or emails—when your grandma sent that sweater for your birthday, when your best friend planned all the travel for your summer trip. In those situations, people are often expecting, or at least aren't super surprised, to get a "thank you" in some form. That's why a "you're awesome" note stands out! It's less transactional, and more spontaneous and personal. Use your note to tell a close family member how much you cherish the time you went out to breakfast together. Or your friend how much their sense of humor means to you. When you make other people happy, it makes you happy too.

## FOLLOW THE STORY IN YOUR HEAD

So much stress in life is related to stuff that hasn't even happened. For example, when you're worried about oversleeping tomorrow morning, or wondering if the sniffles you've been having will turn into a full-blown cold that keeps you home all weekend. You worry about "What if?" and what "could" and "should" happen in the future—which gets in the way of feeling truly happy in the here and now. Instead, play out the full story of whatever is making you stressed. If you do get sick, what will actually happen? "Well," you think, "I'll feel terrible, and I might have to stay in bed all day or take medicine..." Okay, then that's what you'll do! Worry about it if it actually happens; in the meantime, focus on the here and now to feel a little less stress, and a lot more happy.

## EAT BREAKFAST

Eating a nutritious breakfast sets up your day—and your mood—for success. Not only does breakfast provide you with energy and boost your metabolism, it's also an opportunity for some much-deserved self-care. Nurturing yourself in this way creates a ripple effect for your happiness and productivity levels. So eat up!

## INTERVIEW A FAMILY MEMBER

Don't let your history fade away forgotten; take the initiative to interview your loved ones to learn about different stories or significant events. Ask about their childhood, any relatives or ancestors from other countries, travels, educational experiences, etc. You'll feel connected to your genealogy and the family members you interview—connections that will have a huge impact on your overall happiness. Plus, you may learn something surprising.

## KISS SOMEONE

Kissing can make anyone feel good. It releases a whole bunch of chemicals that activate the parts of your brain that manage pleasure, and also lowers stress levels and blood pressure. So if you're looking to lift your spirits in a matter of seconds, have a little make-out sesh.

## KEEP A PROMISE

Keeping promises, both to yourself or other people, promotes self-esteem and makes you feel happy with your life, as you are living according to an important value. After all, being a person with integrity matters, and how you follow through on what you say you're going to do impacts your relationships and the way you see yourself. The next time you vow to do something, do it! It's a simple way to build trust and feel good about who you are.

## SKIP THE SMALL TALK

We've all been stuck in one of those painful situations: The conversation feels awkward or even forced, and you turn to boring, meaningless topics just to avoid silence. It's tiring! Instead, take the opportunity to either ask a deeper type of question and possibly open the door to a more meaningful interaction—or practice getting comfortable with silence. You'll be happier for it, because you'll either connect with someone new on a deeper level or you'll give yourself a chance to relax without the pressure to fill a silent moment.

## PRAY TO A HIGHER POWER

No matter what faith tradition or spiritual beliefs you follow, praying to a higher power can reduce stress and build resilience. It also makes you feel more connected to the world around you, which impacts your overall happiness.

Happiness comes from living as you need to, as you want to. As your inner voice tells you to. Happiness comes from being who you actually are instead of who you think you are supposed to be.

——

**SHONDA RHIMES,**
TV producer and author of *Year of Yes:*
*How to Dance It Out, Stand in the Sun and Be Your Own Person*

## WINDOW-SHOP

As awesome as it feels to purchase that sleek pair of boots or trendy new jacket you've been lusting after, sometimes window-shopping can be super fun on its own. Strolling casually through stores, by yourself or with friends, is a way to browse guilt-free, while sticking to your budgeting or saving goals. You can think about what you like and don't like and look for low-cost alternatives later on, or make a mental list of what to save up for! Another option is filling up your online shopping cart without clicking the "check out" button. Either way, you still experience a bit of a "shopper's high" and enjoy the thrill of hunting for the perfect items.

## MEAL PREP

Prepping breakfasts, lunches, and/or dinners frees up a lot of time for doing the things you really enjoy. Not only do you nix the mental battle of wondering what to eat (and whether you even have the energy to cook) when mealtime rolls around, you're also likely to eat more nutritious options, as they are already made and ready to eat. Set aside a couple of hours to plan your meals for the week and do all the shopping, chopping, and cooking. You can also find easy meal plan and prep guides online, as well as tons of meal prep cookbooks. Both your wallet and your waistline will thank you, and you'll feel good about the effort you put in.

## SNACK ON HEALTHY FATS

You might already know that healthy fats are good for your heart, but they are also good for your mood. Studies show that healthy fats reduce the symptoms of anxiety and depression—a perfect reason to add foods like salmon, chia seeds, extra-virgin olive oil, and nuts into your diet.

## APPLY A TEMPORARY TATTOO

Switch up your look for a couple days—or weeks—with a temporary tattoo. It's super fun, and a good way to test what you like before exploring the real deal! Most options cost just a few dollars, and there are tons of options, from simple floral designs and text to full sleeves and detailed images. Relish expressing yourself with body art, no strings attached.

## SET A GOAL

Think about the things that might be getting in the way of your happiness right now and set a small goal to help you feel happier. For example, if loneliness has been getting you down, set a goal to make one new friend in the next month. And if a bad diet is making you feel sluggish and negative about your body, make it your goal to check out a nutrition class at your local hospital or gym. Make it something simple and attainable that you can do now.

## GET INTO A STATE OF FLOW

When you're one hundred percent focused on an activity, the time just seems to fly by. And as you work, you feel more and more energized and engaged, while filling up the space where negative thoughts or feelings might otherwise creep in. This is what psychologists call "flow": a mental state of being that occurs when you commit your mind completely to something (like running a 5K or drawing a picture). The more time you spend in a state of flow, the less time you have for thoughts that bring you down.

## RECOGNIZE SOMEONE ELSE'S WIN

Celebrating others' triumphs—especially in those instances when it feels easy to get caught up in envy—builds optimism and helps you practice kindness and affirmation. Plus, when it's you on the receiving end of a job well done, you want the people in your life to support you, right?

## LISTEN CLOSELY

Nurturing the different relationships in your life is a huge part of happiness, and giving someone your full attention is an easy way to improve your connection and promote better communication skills overall. When people feel like they are being heard, they hold more positive emotions toward you. So lend an ear: You'll be surprised by how far it can go for everyone involved.

Even a happy life cannot be without a measure of darkness, and the word "happy" would lose its meaning if it were not balanced by sadness.

**CARL JUNG,** psychiatrist

To love someone fiercely,
to believe in something with your whole
heart, to celebrate a fleeting moment in time,
to fully engage in a life that doesn't come
with guarantees—these are risks that involve
vulnerability and often pain....I'm learning that
recognizing and leaning into the discomfort of
vulnerability teaches us how to live with
joy, gratitude, and grace.

**BRENÉ BROWN,**
researcher and author of
*The Gifts of Imperfection*

# BE VULNERABLE

Being vulnerable can be scary: It's a place of uncertainty and complete openness that would make anyone feel out of their comfort zone. And that's a good thing—no, really! Vulnerability is what opens the door to new experiences and deeper connections that lead to a happiness you otherwise would have missed out on. Think about the best things in life: love, friendship, adventure. They all involve putting yourself out there—taking a chance on something, where you might feel tempted to play it safe.

So how do you practice vulnerability? Start by noticing when you feel hesitant to do or say something, out of fear that it might not work out. Maybe you have a joke to share but worry no one will laugh. Or you consider skipping a party because you won't know many people there. Ask yourself: "What if it goes well?" What might you miss out on in *not* taking the risk? In other words, you are identifying when fear is trying to run the show—and challenging it. That mental shift from the negative "what ifs" to the positive ones will help you in putting yourself out there—and inviting happiness into your life.

## HUG A LOVED ONE

Receiving a supportive hug feels amazing, whether you're going through a tough time or just need a little boost. Within seconds, it produces a "cuddle" hormone (yes, that's a real thing!) related to higher oxytocin chemicals and lower levels of cortisol, both of which help minimize stress and promote joy. And as a bonus, research also shows that it's good for your heart, and keeps cold symptoms at bay.

## MAKE A VISION BOARD

Research suggests ambition makes you happier, so get the ball rolling (and beat any negative thoughts about the future) by creating a vision board! Think about your goals—places you want to travel, things you want to accomplish, skills you'd like to learn—grab a big piece of poster board, and start covering it with images related to those goals. You can print out pictures online or cut them out of old magazines. Be sure to hang your vision board somewhere you will see it regularly.

## FINISH A PROJECT

A lingering unfinished project, whether it's a book you're halfway through or reorganizing your bedroom, can be a surprising source of stress and negative feelings. Finish it up—or get rid of it. This will help you follow through on what really matters to you and avoid procrastinating on stuff that isn't important! You'll feel good about checking something off your list, and even better about finishing what you started.

### INVEST IN A CHEAP THRILL

A cheap thrill is anything fun that doesn't require a lot of time or money. They are an easy way to bring more joy into your life. Try to add a couple of cheap thrills to your week: Flirt with the barista at your favorite coffee shop, check out a new bestseller at the library, or indulge in a heaping ice cream cone with all the extras. The point is to give yourself permission to relish whatever small joys make you happy, without any guilt.

### REDEEM A VOUCHER OR COUPON

Anytime you're able to save an extra 10 percent on a purchase, or use a gift card for an item you've been eyeing for months, it gives you a little jolt of joy. It's also super satisfying to snag a good deal. Use up any vouchers or coupons you have to get rid of unnecessary clutter, save cash, and feel good instantly.

### CHECK THE THERMOSTAT

Overly cold or hot temperatures can influence your mood! While Mother Nature is out of your control, you *can* keep an eye on your indoor climate and adjust it to a temperature that you feel most comfortable in. You might love a chilly home where you can layer comfy sweatshirts and light a few candles for atmosphere. Or maybe you think a toasty household is optimal. Either way, change the temperature for an easy mood boost.

**WHAT WE SEE** depends mainly on

**WHAT WE LOOK FOR.**

When we turn our eyes to the sky, it is

in most cases merely to see whether it is likely to rain.

In the same field the farmer will notice the crop,

geologists the fossils, botanists the flowers,

artists the coloring, sportsmen the cover for the game.

Though we may all look at the same things,

it does not at all follow that we should see them.

**JOHN LUBBOCK,** author of *The Beauties of Nature
and the Wonders of the World We Live In*

# LIST THREE THINGS YOU'RE THANKFUL FOR

Quick: In the next sixty seconds, make a list of three things you feel grateful for right now. They can be anything from the practical—"my comfy bed"—to the emotional: "I did my best today." There are no right answers, so don't overthink it; just write. When you are done, go over the list. How do you feel now, thinking about these things, versus before you made the list? Better, right?

Studies show that gratitude practices lead to improved mood, better sleep, higher self-esteem, and more generosity toward other people. In putting pen (or pencil) to paper and listing things you are thankful for, you are forcing your attention to shift from the worries or frustrations that have got you down to the things worth feeling happy about. The best part? It's totally free, and you can do it anywhere, anytime! You can jot a few down in an old notebook, or type them out on your phone to reread whenever you need a boost. You don't have to write exactly three things, either. Just one—or a dozen, if the inspiration strikes—will do the trick. Even if you're feeling more "fake it till you make it" than actually thankful, the act of writing things down can create a genuine sentiment of gratitude. It's like exercise: You may not want to go for a run at first, but you feel a lot better once you start moving. Psychologist and author Robert A. Emmons calls the concept "Velcro": If you actively embrace gratitude, it is more likely to stick. Think of your list as that piece of Velcro, helping you catch more good vibes.

## WRAP YOURSELF IN A SOFT BLANKET

Covering yourself up with a blanket—whether you prefer a plush throw, knitted quilt, or weighted option—makes you feel safe and relaxed. Not only does it remind you of how you might have snuggled up (or been tucked in by a parent) as a kid, but the weight and feel of the blanket also signals your brain to produce more serotonin, which reduces anxiety and lifts your mood. Wins all around! So wrap yourself in your favorite blanket and let the warm, cozy vibes take over.

## SAY "I DON'T"

Saying no instead of yes can come with heavy feelings of guilt—even when you have a good reason to. One hack that makes declining something easier? Turning it into an "I don't" statement. For example, if a friend asks you to go out on a weeknight, say, "I don't go out during the week. But I'd love to make plans for next weekend!" This approach gives you agency over your actions: You're not skipping plans because of some other external factor, but because you're staying true to what you want or need in that moment. Being more authentic around how you do and don't spend your time is powerful. Instead of giving an automatic "yes" and then feeling resentful or hesitant later on, you can feel happy that you honored a healthy boundary. And you'll have more time and energy for what brings *you* joy.

### REROUTE A NEGATIVE PATTERN

Ruminating on negativity keeps you from feeling happy. It can also send you into a downward spiral of even more negativity. Notice when you start to veer toward overthinking or cynicism. Take a mental step back to regroup and shift your attention elsewhere, like going for a run or calling a friend.

### PLAY A FAVORITE ALBUM

Music that you love signals your brain to release dopamine, those feel-good chemicals crucial to happiness. Whether you use a record player or online playlist, playing your favorite album is an instant pick-me-up.

### LOOK AT FAMILY PHOTOS

Family photos represent your heritage. They inspire a sense of pride in who you are and where you came from. They also spark happy feelings as you relive (and maybe even share!) hilarious and beloved memories—like the time your dad backed the car into the mailbox, or when your grandmother baked that epic chocolate cake.

### DOWNLOAD A SHORT MEDITATION

Research shows that regular meditation actually rewires your brain to quiet hyperactive thoughts and strengthen your ability to focus on the positive things, like what makes you happy. And you don't need to devote a lot of time to it, either! Check out an easy ten- or fifteen-minute meditation for immediate benefits.

### REMEMBER A HAPPY MOMENT

Reflecting on past memories is proven to make you significantly happier; in other words, you have full permission to pull a #ThrowbackThursday whenever you like! No need to record or post something, either: You can simply reminisce about a happy time (like that dinner party with friends last weekend, or your favorite holiday traditions) to feel the warm fuzzies.

### FEEL THE SUN ON YOUR FACE

Sunlight releases serotonin, which boosts your mood and balances out the amount of melatonin (the hormone that regulates sleepiness) in your body. Anytime you're trying to steer clear of an afternoon slump, or just need a boost, get outside and soak up a few rays to feel happy and energized.

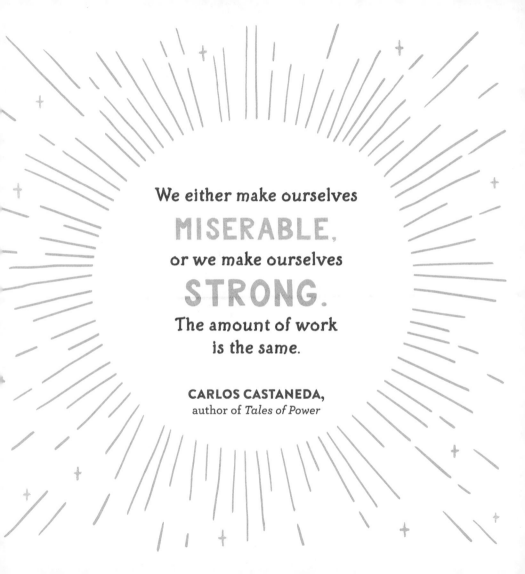

We either make ourselves

**MISERABLE,**

or we make ourselves

**STRONG.**

The amount of work
is the same.

**CARLOS CASTANEDA,**
author of *Tales of Power*

### FLIP THROUGH A CATALOGUE

Instead of immediately throwing out that mail catalogue, take a look to see if anything inspires you. You can even check out e-versions for your favorite companies. Looking for inspiration provides a jolt of happiness as you explore new possibilities for your home, wardrobe, career, and more. It's like window shopping, but in the comfort of your own home!

### GO FOR AN EVENING STROLL

Walking during sunset or against a backdrop of moonlight offers a unique experience: The world is quieter. It's a nice way to decompress after a long day as you reflect on the things you feel grateful for or excited about. The fresh air and exercise can also aid digestion and help you sleep better, making your evening even more relaxing.

### BUY NEW OFFICE SUPPLIES

There's something invigorating about having crisp notebooks, fresh highlighters and pens, and color-coded folders—whether you are in a class or a workspace. You get to envision a successful future and create a sense of order in the present. It's also a way to express your personality with a flashy gold stapler or sticky notes in your favorite color.

## PAY IT FORWARD

Paying forward acts of kindness makes you feel good inside and releases a hormone called oxytocin that lowers blood pressure and stress levels. It also encourages a sense of connection to the world around you. You don't need a ton of time or money, either: Keep the good vibes going by covering the coffee order or toll fee of the person behind you, or finishing a chore for your significant other.

## CREATE A LIST OF WHAT FUELS YOU

Knowing what revs you up—what makes you feel empowered and excited about life—helps you focus your energy toward the opportunities and activities that make you happy. Spend some time thinking about what these things are, and create a list. Start by considering what you could talk about for hours on end, or what motivates you to get out of bed in the morning. These can be things that are simple, like healthy eating, or more in-depth, like animal rights.

## EMAIL YOURSELF A HAPPY STORY

The next time you read a story that brings a smile to your face, send it to your inbox with the subject line "Happy Story!" and save it for a later date. It could be an adorable tale of kids doing cute things, a donation that had a huge impact, or a lost pet reuniting with its owner. Reread the stories whenever you need a lift. (Pro tip: Some publications do weekly roundups of the best human interest stories!)

## FIND A QUIET SPACE

Think about how much quiet time exists in your day-to-day—when there's no music playing, no TV show in the background, no ongoing hum of cars speeding down the street. It's important to carve out dedicated moments of pure quiet, where you can ditch the devices and distractions in favor of silence. Consider it a happy pause for your brain to chill out and refocus. If you're feeling a little scattered, try to find a peaceful moment all to yourself: Skip the podcast on your commute home in favor of some natural downtime.

## WATCH A FUNNY VIDEO

Did you know that it is scientifically proven that a funny video can make you significantly happier? It's true! Whether you're bored, stressed, or just looking for a little lift, humor (along with anything that makes you go "aww") will make you feel better. How? Anytime you experience positive emotions, your brain produces dopamine—that feel-good hormone that keeps the positive vibes going. So go ahead: You have full permission (from science!) to scour the Internet for hilarious memes, cute clips, and comedy specials.

## SHUT OFF YOUR WEEKEND ALARM CLOCK

Getting enough shut-eye matters: When you're overtired, you tend to feel moody and unfocused. And while experts recommend six to eight hours each night, sometimes it can be hard to squeeze them in consistently. Luckily, you can still catch up on your Zs by sleeping in on the weekend. After a long week of 6 a.m. wake-up calls, shut off your Saturday and/or Sunday morning alarm in favor of an extra hour (or three) of sleep. Be sure to keep your phone away from the bed as well, so you're not tempted to start scrolling early and count it as "sleeping in." You'll feel refreshed and ready for another busy week ahead.

## GO FOR A HIKE

There's something appealing about hearing the crunch of leaves under your feet as you concentrate on stepping over loose rocks and muddy sticks. Hiking offers a fun chance to be out in nature, surrounded by trees and fresh air instead of endless emails and text notifications. It helps you stay in the present moment as you focus on your environment, reducing stress and giving a lift to your mental health. You can go full-blown hiker mode with utility boots, a backpack full of extra water and snacks, and a mountain to conquer—or just check out a nearby trail or local state park for shorter, casual options closer to home.

If you suddenly and unexpectedly

feel joy, don't hesitate. Give into it....

Joy is not made to be a crumb.

**MARY OLIVER,**
poet and author of *Swan: Poems and Prose Poems*

# BELIEVE IN ABUNDANCE

When you think about happiness, you might automatically focus on what you don't have: more money, a better car, perfect skin. Or you're on the lookout for what *could* happen to make you unhappy in the future: The person you just matched with on that dating app might eventually ghost you, or you may lose your debit card. It's a default reaction of scarcity that can become a habit, keeping you from feeling truly happy.

Fortunately, with a little intent, you can reroute this mindset! Every time your thoughts start to go toward a negative conclusion, pause. Take note of where your mind is headed (without judgment) and then make the choice to believe in what is good in your life—and what is going to be good in the future. You can come up with a phrase to recite to yourself to help solidify the decision, like, "I believe in the abundance that surrounds me." You can also picture all of the things there are to be grateful for and count them off in your head. By putting faith in what you have, you'll invite even more joy into your world.

### CHECK OUT A FARMERS' MARKET

Supporting a farmers' market in your community can help you feel more connected to the foods you eat, and help you make sustainable choices that keep your body happy too. Knowing where and who your food comes from is a good feeling, and seeing some of the work that goes into it gives you more appreciation for that food.

### MAKE NOISE

Ever notice how little kids love to whoop and stomp around? They aren't afraid to make plenty of noise, and they're onto something: It's so freeing and energizing to let yourself get a little loud! So make some noise. Live authentically and forget about your "inside voice" once in a while (when others are out of earshot, of course).

### HIGH-FIVE SOMEONE

High fives go hand in hand (literally!) with positive moments, like celebrating a win, saying hello, acknowledging someone's hard work, or giving a little encouragement to a friend. And if you're alone, there's no shame in giving yourself a high five to commemorate an achievement—or just celebrate yourself. It's an instant mood-booster!

## RUN A MILE

Studies prove that running can do wonders for both your physical health and mental state. Along with building stronger bones and a vigorous heart, it also helps to clear your mind and lower stress levels, leading to more happiness overall. So hit the treadmill or head outdoors for a short mile run.

## START YOUR MORNING RIGHT

The way you start each day has a huge effect on your mood going forward. Think about the difference between a morning where you hit snooze five times, forget to pack a lunch, and throw on a wrinkled shirt—versus one where you wake up early, drink a glass of water, and have the time for a short activity like journaling mindfully. How you tailor your own morning routine is entirely up to you, but picking things that serve your body, mind, and spirit are crucial to cultivating happiness.

## PICK THREE THINGS TO ACCOMPLISH

Most people don't finish everything on their to-do list every day—usually because there are so many things on it! Instead of feeling overwhelmed or like you aren't putting a dent in your to-dos, limit your daily list to three core objectives: the stuff you absolutely, 100 percent want (or need) to accomplish that day. You'll feel more capable of tackling what you need to do, and even happier when you see the results of focusing on what's most important to you.

### BUY NEW SOCKS AND UNDERWEAR

Undergarments don't last forever! In fact, you should really replace them every six months to a year—especially if you notice something doesn't fit like it used to, or is stretched, faded, or worn out. Invest a little time and money into updating the basics; you'll feel refreshed and put-together. It may even inspire you to take another look at the rest of your wardrobe and what items might not be helping you feel confident and happy.

### WATCH A MUSICAL

Live theater—the real deal on Broadway or a recorded performance—offers something unique to the usual movie. You're able to enter another world, leave behind any worries, and deep-dive into a new perspective or setting. Add catchy show tunes and powerful monologues, and you can't help but feel uplifted.

### APPLY A FACE MASK

The beauty of a face mask is that you can't really multitask or speed through it. It's a chance to slow down, pamper yourself, and relax as your skin absorbs the nutrients. You can choose an inexpensive drugstore mask, a more luxe option, or even make your own at home. Your face will feel hydrated, and you'll be happy you took a little time to treat yourself.

## MAKE YOUR BEDDING EXTRA COMFY

Considering you spend a third of your life sleeping, it's worth making your bed as comfortable as possible. Buy the softest sheets you can find, and have a flannel or fleece set on hand for the colder months. Add a mattress topper with a padded mattress cover for more plushness, plus a down comforter or cozy quilt. (Seriously, this is your excuse to be as extra as you want.) Sleep happy!

## ESTABLISH A STRESS-RELIEF PLAN

The second you start to feel stressed or anxious, what do you do? Maybe freak out a little? Or completely shut down? Not anymore: It's time to make a plan! Think about activities that help turn your mood around immediately, like spraying lavender mist on your hands, counting to ten, or pulling up that funny *Instagram* account that always makes you laugh. Create a list of these quick fixes and stock up on any supplies you need so you are always ready to kick stress to the curb.

## RE-EVALUATE YOUR RELATIONSHIPS

A huge part of happiness is nourishing the relationships that lift you up—and letting go of the ones that bring you down. Take a look at the different relationships in your life and reflect on how each one makes you feel. Are there any you might need to reconsider?

It's funny: I always imagined when I was a kid
that adults had some kind of inner toolbox
full of shiny tools: the saw of discernment, the
hammer of wisdom, the sandpaper of patience.
But then when I grew up I found that life handed
you these rusty bent old tools—friendship,
prayer, conscience, honesty—and said,
"Do the best you can with these, they will have
to do." And mostly, against all odds, they do.

**ANNE LAMOTT,**
author of *Traveling Mercies: Some Thoughts on Faith*

# SPEND TIME WITH A FRIEND

Whether you have a deep bench of soulmate friends from years past or you're branching out with a new squad, friendship is a key part of happiness. With your friends, you can give and receive support, laugh, reflect on the serious stuff, bond over adventures, and stay active—all of which improve your mood, keep stress in check, and boost your physical health too.

Schedule a day, afternoon, or even a five-minute coffee break to hang out IRL with a good friend. You can spend the time catching up and reminiscing about good times, sharing the personal struggles you've both been facing recently, or enjoying a fun activity together. Maybe you both love hiking, or there's a beginners' painting class you've been meaning to try. No matter how you choose to pass the time, you (and your friend) will walk away feeling on top of the world. You may even make a habit of scheduling regular get-togethers to keep your connection strong no matter where life takes you.

## GROW A GARDEN

Planting a garden, whether in your backyard, on a windowsill, or in a patio space, is extremely rewarding. Tending to the plants and watching them grow under your care makes you feel happy, and you'll love having fresh produce within arm's reach (if you choose to grow veggies) or different fresh flavors to enhance your meals (if you grow herbs). Plus, you save time and money spent at the grocery store!

## EXPLORE REIKI HEALING

Reiki, an ancient form of Japanese energy healing, uses special hand placements to release negativity and promote total wellness in your body. You can learn Reiki healing movements online to use on yourself, or enjoy a Reiki massage at a spa.

## REFLECT ON A MISTAKE

So you made a mistake—you're only human! Instead of dwelling on what you feel you did wrong, reflect on any lessons you can learn from it. The goal isn't to be perfect, but to grow from your mistakes. Seeing the positive side to a tough situation is key in manifesting happiness no matter what life throws your way.

### FIND A NEW PERSONAL SCENT

Certain scents are linked to happy feelings (and more self-confidence!). Note what you already gravitate toward: the scent of the apple hand soap in your bathroom, the fragrance of a rosebush, or the smell of freshly baked cookies. Then, use those cues to guide you toward perfumes or colognes that incorporate those scents.

### BLAST MUSIC IN THE CAR

Listening to loud music in a small space like your car makes you feel like you're in the song itself. It gets you pumped up and instantly turns your mood around. Turn up the radio and let the music work its magic.

### SEE A COMEDY SHOW

Live comedy events are one-of-a-kind experiences: You laugh out loud and share in great jokes with others, lowering your stress levels and releasing those feel-good endorphins. Want the chance to go onstage and land a joke of your own? Some venues also have open mic events!

### HOLD SOMEONE'S HAND

It seems like such a small thing, but the act of holding hands can make you incredibly happy. It strengthens your bond with another person, and makes you feel safe and loved. The physical touch on the nerve endings in your fingertips also relieves pain and stress. Take the hand of a friend, partner, or family member, and hold on.

### SING OUT LOUD

Singing is a workout for your lungs and vocal cords that strengthens your immune system and sends more oxygen to your brain. Singing also distracts you from whatever's on your mind. Best of all, when you sing, your brain releases endorphins that make you feel happy; you can belt a tune out loud on your own or harmonize with a friend!

### LEARN CPR

CPR training isn't just for medical professionals; it's for anyone who wants to be prepared should someone need immediate help. It's also a way to feel empowered and confident in yourself and your abilities. A CPR course literally teaches you how to save a life!

## ATTEND A RELIGIOUS SERVICE

Being part of a spiritual community can make you feel happier with your life and more connected to a higher power. Having some form of faith, whether traditional or New Age, also supports your ability to handle the unexpected ups and downs of life.

## LOOK AT PICTURES OF CUTE BABIES

Also known as "the power of puppies," looking at pictures of cute babies (either human or animal!) is proven to relieve stress and boost your mood. Experts have also found that it improves your ability to execute detailed tasks, so you have full permission to take a break from whatever you're doing to prioritize that adorable kitten video.

## JOIN A BOOK CLUB

Meeting with other readers to dissect the latest bestseller is a great excuse to obsess about something you love, and also form relationships with people who share a common interest. You can make new friends, explore all kinds of topics, and stay sharp on current events and what's popular.

When I find myself focusing overmuch on the anticipated future happiness of arriving at a certain goal, I remind myself to "Enjoy now." If I can enjoy the present, I don't need to count on the happiness that is (or isn't) waiting for me in the future.

**GRETCHEN RUBIN,** author of *The Happiness Project: Or, Why I Spent a Year Trying to Sing in the Morning, Clean My Closets, Fight Right, Read Aristotle, and Generally Have More Fun*

# ENJOY THE PRESENT

It's true: Focusing on the here and now leads to more happiness. However, it can seem easier said than done; your mind wanders to a stressful situation from two months ago, or you find yourself thinking, "Is it Friday yet?" In fact, psychologists say the average person is somewhere other than the present for half the time they're awake every day. And when you are not fully in the present, you miss out on what is happening right in front of you.

Of course, paying attention feels easier during life's more thrilling moments: an exciting concert, a skydiving trip, a date with someone you've been admiring from afar. You naturally want to slow time down and live in the moment! But that's only a small part of your life. Most of your life is in the little moments that happen every day, and experts agree that that's where the magic happens. By focusing on each minute as it unfolds, you can fully appreciate and feel happy in it.

So how do you practice living more in the present? Start by noticing when your thoughts go toward the past or future. You can even track how often this happens on a given day, to shed light on just how much of the present you typically miss. And once you feel yourself thinking about the past or future, make the conscious decision to refocus on the here and now. Say a little mantra, take a deep breath, or zero in on a specific element of your surroundings. Over time, staying present will become more automatic.

## RECITE AN AFFIRMATION

Affirmations are personal phrases that typically start with the words, "I am" followed by an action phrase or positive trait. It can be something you're working on, like getting out of your comfort zone ("I am brave") in order to build up your confidence. Or it can be a simple reminder to love yourself ("I am going to treat myself like a friend."). Say one affirmation every day and manifest your own happy reality.

## MEMORIZE A RANDOM FACT

It's extremely rewarding to know the answer to a random question or to impress friends, family, and even strangers with unique facts. Plus, it's just fun to learn something interesting! Keep a piece of trivia in your back pocket, like which musical is the longest-running on Broadway (*The Phantom of the Opera*), how much the most expensive car in the world sold for (a Rolls-Royce Sweptail at $13 million), or how many seconds the longest recorded chicken flight is (thirteen).

## EAT A BANANA

Bananas aren't just a delicious snack: They are also full of tryptophan, a chemical your body translates to serotonin for a boost in mood and energy. Tryptophan also helps regulate blood sugar, preventing larger mood swings. Plus, since they are high in antioxidants, bananas protect you from disease; they also keep you feeling full, thanks to all the fiber.

## TAKE A SPIN CLASS

Indoor cycling classes are a serious workout: They're good for your heart, tough on your muscles (in the best way!), and send endorphins straight to your brain. Try a stationary bike at your local gym, or take a spin class to give your mind and body an extra challenge.

## PRACTICE 4-7-8 BREATHING

This intentional breathing exercise teaches you how to relax while bringing a huge dose of oxygen into your lungs and tissues. It also functions as a way to keep negative thoughts and feelings in check, creating the space for happiness to take their place. To practice 4-7-8 breathing, first inhale through your nose as you count to four. Hold your breath for seven seconds. Then, exhale for eight seconds through your nose. Repeat until you feel better.

## TRY A CHANGE OF SCENERY

If you're feeling down or struggling to stay positive, a change of scenery can be just the thing to adjust your attitude. Going someplace new gives you an opportunity to explore, get away from your regular routine, and view things through a fresh perspective. You can switch things up temporarily, like taking a more scenic route to work, or more permanently, like moving into a new home.

## STRING UP SOME LIGHTS

String lights aren't just for the holidays or outdoor patios. You can throw up Edison bulbs or colorful twinkle lights on a stair railing, around your living room, across your bedroom headboard, or anywhere else you choose for a little fun and additional coziness in your space. It brightens up your home *and* your mood.

## GIVE DINNER A THEME

No, not the kind of theme where you need decorations, costumes, or fancy food (though you can definitely host a themed dinner party if you like!). Rather, consider making your life easier by giving regular dinner nights a theme, like pizza Fridays, taco Tuesdays, pasta Thursdays, or breakfast Mondays. Pick a theme, grab the ingredients, and feel a little less stressed and a lot happier: You've got a (delicious) plan.

## LEARN A PHRASE IN A DIFFERENT LANGUAGE

Knowing even just a couple of common phrases in a different language is not just a fun way to spend a lazy Saturday: It also allows you to better interact with people around the globe! Use an online translator or phone app to learn the basics, like "Hello," "Thank you," "My name is… " and "How are you?". You'll feel great knowing you can navigate a conversation with someone from another culture.

### HANG OUT WITH A POSITIVE PERSON

Certain people just make you feel energized and uplifted. Their positive attitude makes everything fun—and helps you beat your own negative thoughts and feelings. Hang out with someone who will help you shine your light brightly.

### POUR A CUP OF MATCHA

Matcha is a tasty alternative to the typical cup of coffee. It gives you a helpful boost of energy, and it's great for your mood. Found in the same plant as green tea leaves, matcha is loaded with vitamins and antioxidants that make your mind *and* body feel good. You can buy it in a powder form that is whisked with hot water or milk for an easy, healthy pick-me-up.

### VIDEO CHAT WITH SOMEONE FAR AWAY

Video chat makes it feel like you're hanging out in person—no matter how far apart you may actually be. Schedule a video call with a loved one and have fun catching up. It's much more personal than texting, and gives you the chance to see each other's reactions as you share life updates. If you're feeling down, it's also an easy way to vent any frustrations, or get a friend or family member's advice and support for something that has been weighing on you.

I won't just have a job; I'll have a calling.

I'll challenge myself every day.

When I get knocked down, I'll get back up.

I may not be the smartest person in the room,

but I'll strive to be the *GRITTIEST*.

**ANGELA DUCKWORTH,**
psychologist and author of *Grit: The Power
of Passion and Perseverance*

# PERSIST WITH GRIT

Finding and pursuing your passions is an important part of happiness. After all, they are what make the daily grind worth it! And it requires grit. If you're being "gritty," you're always trying to reflect and improve; you use routines and intentional practices to figure out what matters most to you, and how to get it. When you're feeling unsure of your path, grit also helps you stay the course until you figure out what you need to be happy.

Think of grit like a muscle: You need to exercise it on a regular basis. So how do you exercise grit, exactly? Start by looking at the big picture of whatever you're trying to accomplish, rather than the steps to getting there. For example, instead of "I'm doing ten push-ups today," maybe it's "I'm building strength." On the days when you don't really feel like doing those push-ups, or a lack of results so far has you unmotivated, grit reminds you of what you will gain if you keep going. Use grit to fuel your fire and help you to continue working toward the things that will make you happy.

### SEE A MOVIE BY YOURSELF

Why see a movie on the big screen by yourself? For starters, you can choose whatever seat you want, stuff your face with popcorn without worrying about sharing the bag, and pick the movie you see. Besides, you get to watch the previews in peace and don't have to talk to a soul!

### TAKE A PROBIOTIC

Probiotics, microorganisms found in fermented foods, help balance the good kind of bacteria in your gut and promote digestive health. Research also points to the helpfulness of probiotics in your mental health too. Add foods like yogurt and cottage cheese to your breakfast, or incorporate things like pickles, miso, or sauerkraut to your snacks for a tasty mood boost.

### VOLUNTEER AT A SHELTER

Giving your time to a homeless shelter is a great way to help people in your community, as well as appreciate your own blessings. You can volunteer by serving food, organizing donated clothing, or getting trained to help with counseling or other programs.

## PLAN A TRIP

Research indicates the happiest part of travel involves the planning process. It's because of all the anticipation: contemplating how much fun you're going to have in a new location, looking forward to the different activities on your itinerary, counting down the hours until you can enjoy quality time with your travel partners (or yourself). Give yourself a boost by planning your next adventure! Where will you go? Who do you want to bring with you? What things should you pack or get done before jetting off? Relish the excitement of what lies ahead.

## TRY A SOUND BATH

Rooted in cultures that have long used music and vibration as a form of healing, sound baths are now backed by studies that show they can help manage the parasympathetic nervous system, which regulates stress and anxiety. How does a sound bath work, exactly? First, you sit or lie down in a comfortable position. Then, the instructor (or sound therapist) uses repetitive notes created by gongs, cymbals, or crystal bowls to guide you into a meditative state. As you focus on the music around you, you'll feel any negative thoughts or feelings start to drift away in favor of peace and relaxation. Look online for a yoga studio or sound therapist near you that offers sound bath classes.

### TRY ST. JOHN'S WORT

This herbal supplement is a natural, long-term way of improving your mood by aiding sleep and reducing symptoms of depression and anxiety. St. John's wort can be found in most grocery and health food stores.

### GO TO GROUP THERAPY

Participating in group therapy, which usually involves five to fifteen people, isn't just for people in immediate crisis. The sessions are also a great opportunity to get support from others going through similar issues as you—stress, anxiety, and whatever else may be getting between you and happiness. Fellow participants can offer an unbiased ear and provide insights.

### BREAK A BAD HABIT

Good habits lead to a happy you; likewise, bad habits lead to building feelings of guilt, low self-esteem, and even declining health. Set a goal to break a habit that isn't benefiting you. For example, maybe you have been biting your nails. Grab a piece of hard candy every time you feel the urge, and eventually you won't default to nail-biting anymore.

I feel more and more like myself with each passing year, for better and for worse, and you'll find that, too. Every year, you will trade a little of your perfect skin and your ability to look great without exercising for wisdom and peace and groundedness, and every year the trade will be worth it. I promise.

**SHAUNA NIEQUIST,** author of *Bittersweet: Thoughts on Change, Grace, and Learning the Hard Way*

### ENVISION YOUR IDEAL DAY

What does a perfect day look like to you? Write down as many details about it as you can think of. Now, close your eyes and walk through that ideal day, visualizing all of those little details. How can you bring this day to life? Plan a time to make it happen! And even if you can't create that day in the near future, you'll feel happier just picturing it—and thinking about when you *will* have it.

### TRY PROGRESSIVE MUSCLE RELAXATION

One way to release tension and shake off any negativity is a method called "progressive muscle relaxation." Lie down on your back, and, starting with your toes, practice tightening and then loosening each set of muscles in your body. (Work your way up so you end with your face muscles.)

### DO THE MIRROR CHALLENGE

Model Iskra Lawrence champions the "mirror challenge," a self-love strategy to help cultivate happiness. In this strategy, you look directly at yourself in a mirror and list two to three things you like about yourself. The catch? They can't be related to your appearance. The mirror challenge reminds you of how beautiful you are where it counts most: on the inside.

## LEAVE THE PARTY WHEN YOU'RE READY

For all the people-pleasers worried about leaving a party before the lights come on, remember that it's perfectly fine—and good for your mental health!—to head out when you're actually ready to. One element of happiness is knowing your limits, so if you find that your social battery is nearing zero percent, or you're just ready for some downtime at home, don't feel bad. Give a gracious goodbye, note how fun the event was, and move along.

## MAKE AN ESSENTIAL OIL ROLLERBALL

Certain essential oils like lavender, peppermint, and citrus help relax your body, increase your energy levels, and lift your mood. And when paired with a "carrier" oil like olive oil, almond oil, or coconut oil, these scents can be applied directly to your skin for gentle, effective aromatherapy. Pick up a small glass roller bottle (the kind with a metal roll-on insert) and use a dropper to put ten to twenty drops of an essential oil inside, along with six teaspoons of your carrier oil of choice. Seal and shake the bottle, then tap some of the mixture onto your inner wrists, forehead, or the back of your neck.

## RESIST A COMPLAINT

When you feel the impulse to moan and groan about something, try staying silent instead. You'd be surprised by how small complaints throughout the day can build up to a negative attitude. By practicing resisting that urge, you'll notice how much happier you are when you don't give extra attention to the things that can ruin a good mood.

## WATCH A DOCUMENTARY

Documentaries can be a fascinating way to learn about topics you're unfamiliar with, or dig deeper into the history of a person or cultural moment you've wondered about. The next time you sit down to unwind with a movie, try a documentary—it'll zap boredom *and* spark your curiosity. For an extra boost, pick a feel-good story guaranteed to warm your heart.

## DELETE UNUSED APPS

The apps on your phone or tablet take up digital real estate, and seeing that visual clutter can often make your mind feel cluttered too. Go through each one, and if you haven't used it in the last month, delete it. It's a little pick-me-up that leaves you feeling organized and capable of tackling any larger tasks ahead.

### SLOW DOWN WHILE YOU EAT

Shoveling food into your mouth while scrolling through *Facebook* can feel like a default, but it isn't a very satisfying or enjoyable way to eat a meal. Put the joy back into eating by slowing things down so you can actually savor every bite. You'll have the chance to mindfully notice the different parts of your meal—the smell of the roasted potatoes, the warmth of the steak—and also give your stomach time to digest your food properly.

### SKIP THE SCALE

Many people find themselves linking the number on the scale to how happy they feel. Weigh yourself a little less often (or not at all): Your self-esteem doesn't need the trigger, and besides, science proves that number has little to do with how amazing (or healthy!) you are. By skipping the constant check-ins, you can redirect your attention to the things that are truly important.

### PRIORITIZE INTIMACY

A fulfilling sex life leads to better health and more happiness. Of course, intimacy comes in many different forms, whether that means a light kiss and hug or a trip to the bedroom. Prioritize intimacy that makes you—and your partner—feel good.

Hygge is about an atmosphere and an experience, rather than about things. It is about being with the people we love. A feeling of home. A feeling that we are safe, that we are shielded from the world and allow ourselves to let our guard down.

**MEIK WIKING,** author of *The Little Book of Hygge: Danish Secrets to Happy Living*

# CULTIVATE COZINESS

*Hygge*, meaning "cozy," comes from Danish culture. (And the people of Denmark know what's up: The country continues to be named one of the top three happiest places to live in the world.) It is a focus on intentionally warm, intimate moments and social settings. The goal? To boost happiness through camaraderie and comfort—oh, and to hunker down during the cold months.

No matter where you live, there are opportunities to create a sense of hygge in your own home. You can:

- Play board games with your besties over a big bowl of popcorn
- Get together for a casual patio potluck dinner under sparkly lights
- Throw on a knitted sweater and settle in for some *Netflix* and chill
- Start a Sunday brunch club with your favorite people
- Sit around a fireplace roasting marshmallows

Hygge can be inexpensive and easy—a form of everyday happiness where you prioritize simple pleasures.

## BREAK DOWN SELF-CARE

Nurturing your body, mind, and soul through acts of self-care is an essential part of happiness. But as great as it sounds to spend an entire day (or week) devoted to treating yourself, it can be hard to find time to spare—and you don't really need to take that long to reap the benefits. Make it easier to fit in some much needed self-care by breaking it into shorter moments in your usual routine, like a five-minute meditation after waking up, a walk during lunch, a delicious and healthy meal for dinner, and thirty minutes with a good book before bed.

## STEP OUTSIDE

No matter the weather, getting outside for even just a couple minutes provides a reset for your mood—especially if you spend most of the day cooped up inside in front of a screen. You'll also give your brain a moment to recharge in the fresh air, so you can get back to whatever you were doing with more energy.

## LISTEN TO CLASSICAL MUSIC

Music of any kind has therapeutic benefits, but classical tunes are particularly relaxing for your brain. The calm sounds soothe any anxieties you might be feeling, inviting positive vibes to replace them. And if you're trying to focus on something, playing classical music can drown out any distractions. Put on a little Bach, Vivaldi, or Mozart and let the music carry you to your happy place.

## SET A BOUNDARY

Setting boundaries within the different relationships in your life is crucial to self-love: You're aware of your limitations and able to communicate your expectations around respect and happiness. Think about what boundaries you might have for friends, partners, and family, and consider how well-defined those boundaries are. If you've struggled with setting boundaries, try starting small. Say no to something that might hurt your mental or physical well-being.

## GO OUT FOR A MEAL

Dining out is a great way to bring more joy into your life: You're able to enjoy delicious food that you didn't have to make! You can eat alone and relish in the peace and quiet, or make plans with a group of friends to reconnect over a plate of fries.

## FIND AN INSPIRATIONAL QUOTE

Sometimes it can get a little tough to see the silver lining (or the light at the end of the tunnel) when you're faced with a difficult situation. Hey, life can get pretty crazy! But it can also be pretty awesome, and when you're feeling down, it can help to have a visual reminder of this. Spend some time looking for an inspirational quote (or a few) that lifts your spirits and motivates you to push through the obstacles in your life. Be sure to print it out and frame it, or save it to your phone, so you can look to it whenever you need a boost.

## WEAR A PEDOMETER

You probably already know that exercise directly influences your happiness, and wearing a pedometer is the perfect reminder to move your body as much as possible! Seeing your steps add up on the screen motivates you to sit less and helps you set goals for physical activity. You can wear a Fitbit or smart watch, or use an app on your smartphone.

## RESCUE AN ANIMAL

Is there anything more uplifting than the unconditional love of a pet? We think not. If you're ready to adopt a new best pal, make it happen! Visit a local animal rescue to give a home to an animal in need, and prepare for a lot of happiness to come your way.

## HIRE HELP

Oftentimes, feeling overwhelmed is a big obstacle between you and happiness. After all, life can be pretty chaotic! To make it a bit easier on yourself, and create more room for the things that do make you happy, consider budgeting for extra help—like a house cleaner once a month, an accountant to get you through tax season, or a virtual assistant to handle simple tasks.

## MASSAGE YOUR FEET

Massages aren't just for special occasions at swanky spas: You can do a mini at-home version for free! By pampering your feet, you will soothe any pressure that's built up during the day, and feel good about caring for yourself. Start with a little soothing lotion (olive or coconut oil will also do the trick) and, while holding one foot with both hands, massage your heel and arch. Then, dig your thumbs into the ball of your foot and move them in small circles. Wiggle and stretch your toes for added relief. Repeat with your other foot. For an extra treat, apply a foot mask afterward.

## READ ABOUT SOMETHING POSITIVE

When you're stuck in a bad mood, it can feel like everything around you is negative—which makes you feel even worse. To break the cycle, read something uplifting. Proof that there is good in the world—firefighters rescuing a lost pet from a well, a Good Samaritan giving CPR to save a life, kids visiting a nursing home on Halloween—is just the thing to snap you out of that unhappy spiral and remind you of everything worth celebrating in life. Plus, it's pretty hard not to smile when you're reading about something positive. Some broadcast networks and national magazines have "good news" features about inspirational or funny stories, or you can search for articles online.

Financial peace isn't the acquisition of stuff.

It's learning to live on less than you make,

so you can give money back and have money

to invest. You can't win until you do this.

**DAVE RAMSEY,**
author and radio show host

# INVEST YOUR MONEY WISELY

Whoever said money can't buy happiness wasn't spending it the right way! Research shows that when you invest in experiences instead of things—two tickets to a play with your best friend instead of the newest tech trend—you feel happier in the long run. That's because material items have a shelf life: They're awesome on day one, but over time, they no longer feel special or even interesting. Instead, spend your money on an experience, where you'll create memories that last. You can even invest in services that free up your time for these experiences, like a house cleaner, dog walker, or task assistant.

You'll feel happier when you are able to spend your money on what's really important. Of course, this is different for everyone, so take some time to determine where you would or wouldn't want to spend money on an experience. And, of course, make sure you budget for the necessities first, like bills and emergencies.

### DO TEN PUSH-UPS

A quick set of push-ups is an easy way to release some feel-good hormones in your brain, as well as raise your energy levels. Do them from your knees or feet anytime you need a boost, at whatever speed works for you. They'll get easier over time, too, which will make you feel pretty great about what you're capable of.

### STICK A MOTIVATIONAL NOTE ON YOUR MIRROR

Seeing an empowering message whenever you glance in the mirror is a great reminder to stay positive and treat yourself with kindness. Post a sticky note with a motivational phrase that lifts you up and pushes you to keep moving forward, like "Every day is an opportunity for change," or "You are capable!" As a bonus, leave a similar note in a public restroom to make someone else's day.

### READ A POEM OUT LOUD

Poetry has the power to touch your soul and foster deeper reflection on all kinds of topics. And by reading a poem out loud, your attention is drawn completely to the pace of the stanzas, the specific words chosen, and the images they evoke. In other words, you redirect your thoughts away from any negative feelings or worries— toward something uplifting and inspiring.

### PLAN A MOVIE MARATHON

You've got a free night ahead of you. What do you do? Plan a movie marathon, of course! Grab a blanket, a bubbly soda and popcorn, and pick out a set of films to watch start to finish. Any type of trilogy or movie with a sequel will do the trick. Whether you marathon solo or with friends, it's a fun way to boost your mood and make the night (or day—it's up to you) more interesting.

### TAKE CARE OF YOUR NAILS

Your nails reflect your health, and taking care of them is a simple act of self-care that will make you look *and* feel good. Take some time to trim and file them; don't rush. Then, snip any hangnails and rub a hydrating lotion into each finger and around each nail. Your nails will be happy—and you will be too!

### CALL A HELPLINE

Crisis helplines are free, available with the push of a few buttons, and offer whatever help you may need to feel happy. You can call to vent, work through a tough thought or feeling, or learn about other resources in your area. Keep a list of common helpline numbers on your phone, and don't be afraid to call!

## ORDER GROCERIES ONLINE

Not only will you stick to your actual list and choose healthier options when you buy groceries online, but you'll also get to skip the annoyance of packed stores, long lines, and trying to find a parking spot. It saves you time and money, so you can spend it on the things you really enjoy (and check off a big to-do item without the usual stress). Check out how your local stores handle online orders, as many have same-day pickup or affordable delivery.

## READ A CELEBRITY PROFILE

Online profiles are an awesome way to get to know famous people on a deeper level than what you usually see on social media or TV. You get interesting facts to share with others, and you learn about the doubts and mistakes they have struggled with (they're human too!). You might even find common ground in your own challenges. Either way, it's a fun pastime that provides more perspective and appreciation for your life.

## DO A PILATES EXERCISE

Pilates is a form of exercise that tones your body and helps clear your mind. Through different movements, you engage key muscles in a way that requires complete focus, allowing you to let go of any negative thoughts or feelings. Try an online tutorial or visit a local studio.

"Well," said Pooh, "what I like best—" and then he had to stop and think. Because although eating honey was a very good thing to do, there was a moment just before you began to eat it which was better than when you were, but he didn't know what it was called.

—

**A.A. MILNE,**
author of *The House at Pooh Corner*

### JOG IN PLACE

Running in place isn't just for a warm-up before your workout: You can do it anytime you need an extra dose of serotonin and energy. Start slowly by bending each knee and simply lifting your feet off the ground one at a time, and then work up to a fast-paced jog with high knees. You want to feel out of breath at the end, so aim for at least two minutes of jogging to get your heart racing!

### VISIT A LOVED ONE

Quality time with the people you love directly impacts your mood—especially when you're able to be together in person. Seeing your loved one's face during a conversation, as well as having the ability to embrace or touch them, is a great feeling.

### STEP INTO A SAUNA

A short stint in a sauna can leave you feeling calm and ready to take on the day. In fact, studies show saunas can help lower your blood pressure while increasing your heart rate—both of which contribute to your health and happiness. Your local gym or spa will typically have a sauna you can use.

## MAKE A COLLAGE

Remember that collage you made in art class as a kid? It's time to tap into your creative side and give your mood a boost with this throwback to simpler times! Collages are a fun way to express yourself, and even reflect on and let go of something that has been on your mind. You can cut images and words from old magazines, print things out online, pop on some stickers, paint—the possibilities are endless!

## BUILD A LEGO SET

Tap into the simple joy of being a kid by playing with LEGOs! Beyond being a fun pastime, it helps you nurture creativity, practice self-control, build resilience, and navigate tricky situations—all of which factor into long-term happiness. Pick up a cheap set or dig out your old bricks from storage and tinker around.

## CHECK OUT A POTTERY STUDIO

Turning clay into a mug, bowl, or funky vase is a fun and unique way to beat a bad mood. You're getting into the zone and building something with your hands, which feels good. Plus, you get something new to take home or give as a personalized gift. Sign up for a class in your area.

## REARRANGE YOUR BEDROOM

If you tend to turn into an interior designer when you're in a funk, know that you're not alone: rearranging furniture makes us feel better. Why? It's related to feng shui, an ancient Chinese practice known as the "art of placement." In a nutshell, feng shui involves positioning your decor in ways that harness your energy and boost your mood. To refresh your space and clear out negative vibes, start by moving your bed so it is facing the door (but not in line with it). Hang up your favorite pictures in new spots and change up the items on your desk. Try a few different options for a look that feels right.

## CRY IT OUT

It might sound counterintuitive, but crying is great for your mood! It releases feel-good endorphins and signals your parasympathetic nervous system to focus on rest. Crying also allows you to process your emotions in a healthy way, (literally) washing away stress and negativity. So don't hold back: Find a quiet place to have a good cry. You may even consider putting on a favorite touching movie or song to get the tears flowing. When you're done, you'll feel refreshed and a whole lot lighter.

## WRITE OUT YOUR SCHEDULE FOR THE WEEK

Taking even just five minutes at the beginning of every week to think about what's in store—and what you actually want to do—goes a long way in having a productive and happy week. Slot out time on Sunday evenings or Monday mornings to grab a planner or your smartphone calendar and write down any upcoming appointments, big meetings, work commitments, friend dates, etc. Then, go back through the week and add at least two to three acts of self-care.

## CHOP VEGETABLES

Cutting veggies requires careful concentration: You're using a sharp knife, after all! You're also focused on a single, rhythmic activity that has a clear result. In other words, it feels good to refocus your thoughts on the simple, satisfying task of chopping that onion into perfect chunks for a stir-fry. And if you have any negative energy floating around in your mind or body, you can have some fun releasing it with a few solid thwacks.

## PRACTICE YOGA

Finding happiness can sometimes feel daunting, but yoga gives you a few great tools to help you along the way! It teaches you how to redirect the negative thoughts and feelings weighing you down so you can get into a more positive, empowered mindset. Check out a yoga class or follow along with an easy video online.

Ask yourself: Are you spending your time on the right things? You may have causes, goals, interests.

## ARE THEY EVEN WORTH PURSUING?

**RANDY PAUSCH,**
author of *The Last Lecture*

# READADJUST YOUR PRIORITIES

Picture this: You're getting ready for bed, thinking about the things you didn't do today. Maybe you skipped your morning workout, forgot to call your aunt back, or spent exactly zero minutes on that new creative project you've had in mind. You promise yourself you'll get to it tomorrow, only to run out of time for what's important *again*. Why does this happen? You're likely stuck in reactive mode, responding to whatever urgent activity pops up first, instead of focusing on what you want to accomplish. Hitting refresh on email, checking text messages for the third time in an hour, cleaning out that desk drawer—it all feels productive, but each decision steals time away from your main priorities.

Consider what makes you happy. Ideally, this list should be composed of only the truly important things, like family, physical health, faith, etc. Now, write down all of the things you do during the typical day. Put a star or check mark next to every item in this second list that aligns with your list of priorities. There should be at least one thing you do each day to fulfill a priority. If there isn't, it's time to make an adjustment to your schedule. For example, if spending quality time with your family is a priority, take the time to see or call them. If you want to run up a flight of stairs without losing your breath, you may consider skipping an hour of mindless channel surfing to exercise. Getting clear on your priorities allows you to reclaim your time. That will make you happier!

## TRY ACUPUNCTURE

Whether you're dealing with a headache, back or neck pain, stress, or a case of the blues, this form of traditional Chinese medicine can help you feel healthier and happier! Just be sure to check with your doctor before exploring this option, and seek out referrals for a certified practitioner.

## WATCH A TV SHOW

Nothing gets you out of your own head like watching someone else's story play out on screen. Find a sitcom, sports commentary, travel or cooking show, or a juicy primetime drama to pique your interest and send that bad mood packing. You might discover a new favorite, or even a better appreciation for your own life.

## TAKE DEEP BREATHS

Rather than getting all tied up in the worries or frustrations in your mind, taking deep breaths forces you to pause and check in with your body, refocusing those negative thoughts. As you breathe in and out, envision releasing all of the things that get between you and happiness; feel them evaporate into the atmosphere, leaving fresh, positive vibes in their place.

## MAKE A DOCTOR'S APPOINTMENT

Yes, scheduling a doctor's appointment *will* lead to more happiness. How? It'll help you keep an eye on your physical and emotional health, so you can nip any issues in the bud and learn helpful tips for feeling your best. There's no reason to wait until something feels seriously wrong before looking to a healthcare professional for support.

## USE A BODY SCRUB

Skip the old, boring bar of soap (especially if it's looking a little grimy on your shower shelf) and invest in a body scrub or wash. Look for one with all-natural ingredients and a great smell, then exfoliate away to revitalize your skin and remove dead cells. You'll be glowing inside and out!

## MAKE A BATCH OF SOUP

A warm bowl of broth or hearty pot of chili simmering on the stove is great for your stomach—and your mood. It promotes mindfulness, because you have to slow down to spoon and enjoy every bite. It also serves as the perfect comfort food when you're feeling sick or just down in the dumps.

## CREATE AN AWAY MESSAGE

These days, it feels like a challenge to find a place where you *can't* get Wi-Fi or at least cell service. Give yourself a break for some quality "me time" by scheduling "out of office" or "unavailable" auto-replies. Not only will you feel more relaxed and able to focus on things that make you happy, but it will also help you manage the expectations of others.

## SAVE THE BEST PART OF A TRIP FOR LAST

When you're enjoying time off for a little rest and relaxation, the last day of your trip can sometimes feel like a bummer. Instead of anticipating the return to real life, save a special activity or fun outing for the end! Plan a delicious breakfast, try something new—whatever makes the day feel like a celebration full of good vibes that can keep going.

## RE-EVALUATE YOUR FAVORITES

What activities or habits have been your favorites for as long as you can remember? Just like our bodies are always changing, so are our minds; the things you used to value may no longer fit into your dreams for the future. Take this opportunity to step away from what you "always" do and consider if these still add happiness to your life or are just defaults. You can also use this time to explore new things that might make you happy.

The grand essentials to happiness in this life are something to do, something to love, and something to hope for.

**GEORGE WASHINGTON BURNAP,** Unitarian clergyman and author of *The Sphere and Duties of Woman*

### SURPRISE A SIBLING

Any type of "just because" gift is a sweet way to show someone you care—and lift your own mood in the process. Think of something simple, like a funny book you know your brother will love or a cute stuffed animal for your younger sister. You don't have to spend much money—you can even go the DIY route.

### LOOK OUT THE WINDOW

Staring into space may seem like wasted time, but it's actually a great opportunity to let your mind relax, or to reflect on whatever thoughts pop up. You don't have to be productive; you can just observe the world and tune in to how you're feeling. You'll notice the beauty in an ordinary day while letting go of any negativity that had been weighing you down.

### TIP YOUR SERVER EXTRA

Tipping is more than payment for good service: It's a way to acknowledge the human being behind the job. By adding even a little extra to your tip, you might make your server's day—and boost your own mood in the process.

## VISIT SOMEONE IN THE HOSPITAL

Doing good feels good—it's a fact! And one of the simplest ways you can help is by visiting a sick friend or relative in the hospital. Showing up in good spirits has a ripple effect on that person, and when you see how your positivity lifts your friend or loved one's mood, you will be motivated to keep the happy vibes going.

## FOLLOW A THERAPIST ON SOCIAL MEDIA

Some therapists have a social media presence full of inspirational quotes and helpful wellness tips, so even if going to regular therapy isn't a viable option at the moment, you can follow these experts to learn from afar. Save your favorite posts and look back to them whenever you're feeling down for a free boost no matter where you are!

## THANK A FORMER TEACHER

Think about a teacher or professor who impacted you—someone who encouraged your education, supported the topics you felt passionate about, and made the classroom interesting. Do they know how important they were in your journey? Make a point of telling them! Send a card or email thanking them for being such a wonderful mentor. It's guaranteed to make their day *and* yours.

Health is not just the absence of a disease.

It's an inner joyfulness that should

be ours all the time;

a state of **POSITIVE WELL-BEING.**

**DEEPAK CHOPRA,**
author of *Journey Into Healing*

# CHECK IN WITH YOUR HEALTH

Want to be healthy? Be happy. Want to be happy? Be healthy: The two go hand-in-hand. In fact, research links happiness to a longer life, stronger heart, and better immune system—plus fewer aches, stressors, and diseases over time. When you're happy, you're more likely to take care of yourself and stick to healthy behaviors like eating fruits and veggies, sitting less and moving more, and catching up on your Zs. When you're healthy, you're more likely to feel happy!

Start the cycle off right (or get it back on track) by doing regular body check-ins to pinpoint any areas of your health in need of a little extra TLC. To do a full body check, begin with your feet: How do they look and feel? Any aches or pains? No? Okay, now move on to your ankles and lower legs. Work your way up through your body, ending with your head. Some issues may be fixed with an over-the-counter pain medication, Band-Aid, or patience. Other issues might require a visit to the doctor.

### SIGN UP FOR A ROAD RACE

Road races are a unique way to explore a city and often benefit a nonprofit or charity at the same time. Plus, the exercise gives you a boost of feel-good hormones like serotonin. You can sign up for any length (5K, 10K, half-marathon, etc.) depending on whether you are new to racing (or want to keep a more casual pace) or an experienced runner. It'll give you an exercise goal to work toward and motivation to stay on track.

### CHERISH A MUNDANE MOMENT

Ordinary moments matter; life will pass you by if you don't stop to pay attention! Instead of focusing on just the really good (and really bad), cherish as much as possible. Take in that quiet morning at home, your drive to work, the way the sky looks right now, and so much more. Happiness isn't just in "big" moments.

### FOCUS ON YOUR BREATH WHEN YOU WAKE UP

Rather than reaching for your phone the minute you open your eyes in the morning (we've all done it!), dedicate that moment to a quick morning breathwork session. While you're still in bed, put one hand over your heart and take five deep, slow breaths in through your nose and out through your mouth. This easy exercise will help direct the usual morning's flood of thoughts in a positive, organized way, prepping you for a happy, successful day.

## VALUE YOUR AGE

It's time to let go of outdated stereotypes about certain decades and milestone birthdays. The age you are right now is what matters; you might as well enjoy it! If you feel your thoughts lingering in the past or dreading getting older—at the expense of living up the present—take a moment to appreciate your current age and focus on all the great things you can do to enjoy it.

## PRACTICE WORK-LIFE BALANCE

Work-life balance is more than an even split between hustling and recharging. It's a blend of all the things that make you happy (e.g., fitting in a weekly exercise class), along with the stuff you have to do, like paying taxes. This helps create more satisfaction about the life you're leading, so you can avoid burnout and prioritize what matters most to you. Practice balancing the times you are super productive with a little self-care, either scheduled in as quick sessions or as a full personal day.

## IDENTIFY YOUR INNER CIRCLE

Friendships change as you evolve and grow, and it's important to identify and possibly re-evaluate who's in your inner circle once in a while. Consider whether each person in this circle is genuine and motivates you to be your best, happiest self—and who might be more of a drain on your emotional energy.

I am still determined to be cheerful and to be happy, in whatever situation I may be; for I have also learnt, from experience, that the greater part of our happiness or misery depends upon our dispositions, and not upon our circumstances. We carry the seeds of the one or the other about with us, in our minds, wheresoever we go.

**MARTHA WASHINGTON,**
former first lady of the United States

# REBOOT YOUR "HAPPY" SET POINT

Happiness is a choice. The sales clerk with a giant smile and a bubbly voice, your brother who doesn't get worked up about anything, your dog absolutely l-o-v-i-n-g his daily walk—they are decidedly happy about life! Being happy doesn't happen overnight, though, and depending on who you are, it can require different levels of maintenance, commitment, and bravery. In fact, one theory is that everyone has a happiness "set point" that determines their well-being. When good or bad things happen, you trend upward or downward, but generally you stay around the same level. However, you always have the opportunity to reboot that set point and choose to intentionally seek more happiness.

To refresh your attitude toward happiness, start by thinking about your baseline moods. How do you feel on a typical day? Then, think about what things make you feel happy. Now, lay out some small choices you can make on a daily basis to prioritize those types of activities. These frequent boosts add up over time, raising your happiness set point so you default to a better mood more often.

### COLOR IN A COLORING BOOK

Adult coloring books are an excellent option for creative escape. Consider it art meditation: By focusing on coloring, your brain is forced to let go of any worries, frustrations, etc., and concentrate on the task at hand. It's a fun way to relax and show negativity the door. So grab a set of colored pencils and chill out.

### LEARN CALLIGRAPHY

Writing in calligraphy is a meditative experience that fosters creativity and draws your attention away from negative thoughts or feelings—toward the relaxing, satisfying act of drawing beautiful letters. You can find pre-assembled kits, or purchase individual beginner-level supplies at your local craft store. Check out a class at your local art center or look up an online tutorial and print off a few worksheets to try at home. Then, get in the zone and script away with a little music in the background.

### MAKE A DECISION

There's power in being decisive about what you want, even when you don't totally know how the outcome will play out. You can't help but feel good when you conquer self-doubt, cut through hesitations like "What if?" and "Well, maybe," and say, "This is what I choose." And with every decision you make, it gets easier to continue trusting yourself. You've got this!

Everybody in the world is seeking happiness—and there is one sure way to find it. That is by controlling your thoughts. Happiness doesn't depend on outward conditions. It depends on inner conditions. It isn't what you have or who you are or where you are or what you are doing that makes you happy or unhappy. It is what you think about it.

**DALE CARNEGIE,**
author of *How to Win Friends and Influence People*

### JOIN A SUPPORT GROUP

Support groups give you a safe and encouraging space to talk, whether you're navigating a big life transition or loss, or just feeling down in the dumps. You also have the opportunity to make connections with other people who are going through similar situations and may have unique insights to help you overcome any obstacles between you and happiness.

### WASH YOUR HAIR

Investing in the way you wash your hair is an easy way to put extra pep in your step. Choose a shampoo and conditioner with a scent you love, and give yourself an extra minute to fully scrub your scalp. Consider trying an at-home hot oil treatment or luxe heat repair spray for even more pampering. You'll feel clean and confident.

### DONATE BLOOD

Donating blood has the same benefits as volunteering: You're able to help people in need—and feel good about yourself—through a simple act of service. Look out for local blood drives, or make an appointment at an American Red Cross or hospital.

## LISTEN TO AN INSPIRATIONAL PODCAST

No matter the topic, there's a podcast for it. Listening to podcasts is a great (often free!) way to be entertained or learn about a new subject, and you can listen anywhere: in the car, walking down the street, cleaning house, or waiting in line. Boost your mood in a matter of minutes with an inspirational episode featuring an expert on positive psychology or self-help, or an uplifting story about a personal triumph. Good places to start include *School of Greatness*, *Happier with Gretchen Rubin*, and *TED* podcasts.

## CREATE A BEDTIME ROUTINE

A good bedtime routine helps you fall (and stay) asleep, so you can wake up refreshed and excited for the day ahead. Dedicate at least thirty minutes to winding down before bed; set an alarm on your phone as a reminder. Your bedtime routine can include anything that helps you relax, like reading a book or meditating, as well as the self-care rituals key to a good night's sleep, like washing your face and brushing your teeth. Keep your routine tech-free, so your brain gets "fall asleep" signals instead of "stay awake to scroll through social media" ones.

The most beautiful people we have known
are those who have known defeat, known
suffering, known struggle, known loss, and
have found their way out of the depths. These
persons have an appreciation, a sensitivity,
and an understanding of life that fills them
with compassion, gentleness, and a deep loving
concern. Beautiful people do not just happen.

**ELISABETH KÜBLER-ROSS,** psychiatrist

# FIND THE BEAUTY IN YOUR STRUGGLE

You're happy...minus the fact that you still have six figures of loans to pay off. You're happy...except that you're having a hard time coping with a loss. You're happy...apart from being sick for the second week in a row. Whatever dark period or tough situation you've encountered recently, the truth is that you can still find happiness at the same time. You don't have to wait until a rough patch is over to feel happy.

Psychologist Sonja Lyubomirsky describes happiness like a pie chart with three slices: 50 percent constitutes your genetic "set point," or where you naturally fall in terms of happiness on the typical day; 40 percent is related to intentional activities or behaviors; the remaining 10 percent of the pie is life circumstances. Your ability to live a happy life is entirely up to you. You can't escape adversity or difficulty or sadness, but you can choose what you do with it. Focus on finding the beauty in the situation at hand, instead of rushing ahead to what might happen in the future (or dwelling on what happened in the past).

## HAVE A DAY WITHOUT ANY "SHOULD"S

It's so easy to slip into "should"-ing yourself: "I should've worked out today"; "I should've eaten healthier at lunch"; "I should've asked a question at that meeting." But all those "should"s don't change anything; they only keep you from being happy in the here and now. Give yourself a day where "should"s aren't allowed. As they pop into your head, acknowledge that they are there, and then say, "Not today!"

## SPLURGE ON NIGHT CREAM

Using a night cream or oil before bed feels like a lavish part of your self-care routine, whether you spend five bucks or fifty. Pick something with a refreshing scent and fully tune into the experience as you apply it; notice the feel of the cream and your skin as it is absorbed. It feels good to take care of yourself!

## DO MORNING PAGES

Author and artist Julia Cameron created an activity called "morning pages," where you write three pages as soon as you wake up. Don't overthink it! Just follow your stream of consciousness and get the thoughts down. It'll help clear your mind before you start the day, encourage you to let go of any anxious or unhappy thoughts, and set the stage for inspiration and positivity.

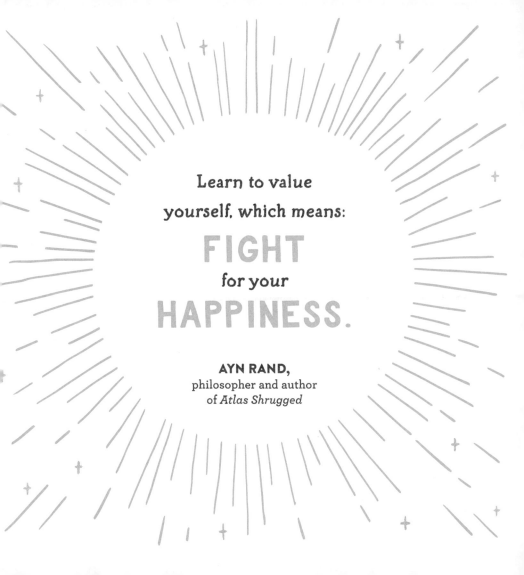

Learn to value
yourself, which means:
# FIGHT
for your
# HAPPINESS.

**AYN RAND,**
philosopher and author
of *Atlas Shrugged*

## PEEL AN ORANGE

Low levels of vitamin C can make you feel tired and even sad. So go ahead and enjoy a fresh orange for a tasty afternoon snack that provides extra perks. Also, the scent of citrus itself gives you a refreshing lift, because it signals your body to produce that "happy hormone," serotonin!

## SLIP INTO AN ICE BATH

Feeling anxious? Redirect those unhappy thoughts to a little positive stress (yes, it is a thing!). Not only will dipping into an ice bath distract you from what has you feeling troubled, but it will also ease any physical tension as well. Plus, it can be pretty empowering to push yourself in a little challenge of mental and physical endurance. See how many minutes you can sit in the ice bath.

## SORT A STACK OF PAPERS

Filing paper—bills for annual taxes, cards from long-distance friends, old homework projects—helps you stay organized. It is also an easy way to boost your mood by easing stress and making you feel productive. And in today's digital world, there's really no reason to keep stacks of paper lying around anyway. Go through the pile and either throw away, label and store, or scan papers to save electronically.

Happiness is the consequence of personal effort.
You fight for it, strive for it, insist upon it, and
sometimes even travel around the world looking for it.
You have to participate relentlessly in the
manifestations of your own blessings.

**ELIZABETH GILBERT,**
author of *Eat, Pray, Love*

## GET A DEEP TISSUE MASSAGE

Stress can lead to chronic pain in your body, which leads to even more stress: It's a vicious cycle! So if your back, hips, or neck have been feeling tense and even achy, find a licensed massage therapist who specializes in deep tissue therapy. They'll focus on any problem areas you may have, eliminating the tension—and the stress along with it.

## SWAP RED MEAT FOR FISH

According to a 2010 study, eating fish regularly protects against depression (thanks mostly to the omega-3 fatty acids). Even more good news? Fish also packs a heart-healthy punch, boosts your brain power, and protects your vision. Consider swapping that red meat for cod, mahi-mahi, or light tuna a couple times a week.

## FLOSS YOUR TEETH

Healthy gums lead to healthy teeth—which lead to a healthy, happy you. Put a sticky note on your bathroom mirror to remind yourself to floss at least once a day to remove the build-up of plaque and lower your risk of heart disease and other complications. And feel proud of yourself for successfully adulting!

Solitude is very different from a "time-out" from our busy lives. Solitude is the very ground from which community grows. Whenever we pray alone, study, read, write, or simply spend quiet time away from the places where we interact with each other directly, we are potentially opened for a deeper intimacy with each other.

**HENRI NOUWEN,** Catholic priest and author of *Clowning in Rome: Reflections on Solitude, Celibacy, Prayer, and Contemplation*

If you look for perfection, you will **NEVER BE CONTENT**.

**LEO TOLSTOY,**
author of *Anna Karenina*

## ACCEPT YOURSELF

There is so much pressure to be perfect—to always say the right thing, meet all deadlines, never forget a birthday, and on and on. And even though you may know deep down that perfectionism isn't real, it's easy to slip into a place of feeling like you're not good enough or bound to fail.

The best thing you can do to feel better? Accept yourself. Instead of dwelling on what you can't change, like the fact that you didn't get that interview or how your sister has a better knack for numbers—focus on accepting the reality of who you are. Embrace your imperfections, because they make you wonderfully unique! How? Start by considering the parts of yourself rooted in negativity and see if you can show yourself a new perspective. For example, let's say you got a speeding ticket last weekend for driving fifteen miles over the limit. Your inner critic might say that you're a terrible driver. But maybe you need to acknowledge that while you were rushing to get to the next place (and should be a bit more careful next time), the fact that you have so much energy and focus is a valuable part of who you are. Learning to accept all of the parts of yourself is a key part of happiness: When you appreciate yourself for who you are, you feel good about life.

# INDEX

# ABOUT THE AUTHOR

**JULIA DELLITT** is a freelance writer whose work has been published by *BuzzFeed*, *Forbes*, Self.com, *Lifehacker*, *Brides*, *The Everygirl*, *Aaptiv*, and more. She graduated from the University of Chicago with a master's degree in religion and literature, and from Augustana College with a degree in English and political science. She lives in Des Moines, Iowa, with her husband and two children. To find out more, visit julmarie.com.